Ciao Italia
IN TUSCANY

To Madeleine,
the best cook!
Buon Natale!
Ciao

2004

ALSO BY MARY ANN ESPOSITO

Ciao Italia

Nella Cucina

Celebrations Italian Style

What You Knead

Mangia Pasta!

Ciao Italia—Bringing Italy Home

Ciao Italia in Umbria

Ciao Italia
IN TUSCANY

Traditional

Recipes from

One of Italy's

Most Famous

Regions

MARY ANN ESPOSITO

St. Martin's Press New York

www.stmartins.com

Design by Kate Nichols

Library of Congress Cataloging-in-Publication Data

Esposito, Mary Ann.
    Ciao Italia in Tuscany : traditional recipes from one of Italy's most famous regions
    Mary Ann Esposito
        p. cm.
    Includes index (p. 325).
    ISBN 0-312-32174-0
    1. Cookery, Italian—Tuscan style.   2. Cookery—Italy—Tuscany.   3. *Ciao Italia* (Television
program)   I. *Ciao Italia* (Television program)   II. Title.

TX723.2.T86E87 2003
641.5945'5—dc21

                                                                          2003046882

10 9 8 7 6 5 4 3 2

Author's Note

This book is the eighth companion cookbook to the television series *Ciao Italia*. It is also the second "traveling cookbook" I've written. Like *Ciao Italia in Umbria*, which focused on that region's cooking, this book is devoted to Tuscany—its food, people, and culture. Within its pages are recipes seen on the series, as well as others. Through recipes, anecdotes, and the passing along of traditonal methods and techniques I picked up while taping in Tuscany, I've tried to share with my readers (and viewers) what traditional Tuscan food has been and, I hope, what it will continue to be.

Contents

Acknowledgments · *xi*

Introduction · *xv*

The Lord and Lady of Spannocchia · *1*

The Mindful Gardener · *5*

When Tuscan Women Cook · *15*

My Big Fat Tuscan Pizza(s) · *27*

The Little Church with the Blue Door · *33*

To Eat Like a Florentine · *35*

The Merchant of Prato's Biscuits · *45*

San Sepolcro's Secrets · *51*

How to Read a Tuscan Menu · *60*

Lucca's Legacy · *63*

Dinner in a Palazzino · *69*

Palazzo Davanzati · *83*

A Taste for Saltless Bread · *89*

A House with a View · *101*

Maria Pia's Pleasing Pisa Paté · *105*

Vineyard Kitchen · *115*

In the Shadow of The Medici · *131*

Practicing *Al Fresco* · *141*

In Michelangelo's Neighborhood · *143*

Sauce Sense · *155*

Signature Sweets of Siena · *165*

A Chef Goes to Tuscany · *181*

Minding My Garden · *193*

A Day for Vin Santo · *211*

The Tuscan Pantry · *213*

Favorite Tuscan Restaurants · *215*

Mail-Order Sources · *219*

Tuscan Food and Wine Web Sites · *223*

English Index · *225*

Italian Index · *231*

Acknowledgments

WRITING ABOUT the food culture of Italy has been a passion and a career of mine for close to twenty years, and all that I have learned I owe to a long list of people both here and in Italy. As with my previous books, I have many to thank for helping me to bring this book to fruition. To our valued underwriters for their financial assistance: John Profaci and the entire Profaci family at Colavita USA, and Jennifer Lionti, assistant marketing director, thank you for the outstanding assistance whenever we needed it, and to Jason Knight at Bella Sera Wines, Venda Ravioli and Alan Costantino, and to Kitchenetc.com, especially Larry Job and Bob Camp.

To friends in Italy, especially Randall Stratton and Francesca Cinelli, thank you for so beautifully accommodating our television crew at Spannocchia. In Florence, thanks to Luciano and Ana Berti, Gioni and Iris Lodovici, and Gian-Andrea Lodovici. In Bignola, thanks to Edoardo Catemario for the beautiful music, and to his wife, Adalgisa, for hosting us and a number of friends in their sweet home. In Siena, thanks to Marco Giacchi for his assistance with filming. In Settignano, thanks to chefs Damiano Miniera and Silvia Miniera, and Heiko Mattern at La Sosta del Rossellino. In San Sepolcro, thanks to Marco Tofanelli for his hospitality at Da Ventura Ristorante. In Montalcino, thanks to Lars Leight, Elizabeth Hoenig, Dante Cecchini, and chef Maria Gorelli of Villa Banfi. In Teverina, abundant thanks to Nancy Harmon Jenkins for allowing me to make and break Tuscan bread with her. In Pisa, thanks to dear friends Maria Pia and Claudio Vitagliano.

Here at home, many thanks to Jane Almeida for introducing me to Spannocchia, to photographer Bill Truslow for driving me around the Tuscan countryside to capture elegant photos, to Donna Petti-Soares, who kept detailed notes of everything that happened in Tuscany and who was our expert transportation and map-reading whiz. To videographer Cindy Jones for a superb job, and to Jeff Spence, our audio specialist, who will go to Italy anytime with me for a gelato. To Paul Lally, executive producer of *Ciao Italia,* for every hat that you wear, I tip mine to you for your consistent elegant work; I would be nowhere without you. To associate producer-director Jennifer Soares for her total dedication to the job. To Michael Jones, Esquire, for his professional advice, and to my dear husband, Guy, for his encouragement and for his careful planning and tending of the *Ciao Italia* garden. To the administration and staff at Channel 36 in Providence, Rhode Island, especially Susan Farmer, David Piccerelli, Bob Knott, and director James Garrett. To the television camera, studio, and kitchen crews for their dedication to making good television. To senior culinarian Donna Petti-Soares, a stickler for details and perfection, and to culinary supervisor and Web librarian Ruth Moore for her superb viewer services. To Scott Saracen and Mike Reilly for postproduction of the series, and Jodi Mesolella for fulfilling cookbook orders. To Steve Shipley for providing our prep kitchen with the best culinary students that Johnson and Wales has to offer, to pastry chef Cindy Salvato for the beautifully displayed "presents," to John Gates for his masterful lighting and his sense of humor, to Leslie Ware for always being there, even in spirit. To Alexandra Iori, who was our Italian ambassador; Becky Soares, for neatly keeping our inventory; to the faithful volunteers who came to wash dishes and do many other daily tasks; and to Panera Bread and Bahjat Shariff for feeding our crew and supplying props. To Donna Lee Del Sesto for all that shopping, and chef Walter Potenza for cooking *nella cucina.* To Kelly Drapeau at the Providence Marriott hotel for providing the *Ciao Italia* crew with many a good night's sleep, and to chef Ralph Conte for his unfaltering presentation of authentic Italian foods. To Home Improvement for the flooring, and Company C for the beautiful rugs, and to Felicia Bebleman at the HearthKit Kitchen Company. To Steve Costantino and Gordon Fox for believing in the series, to Scialo Brothers Bakery, especially Carol Gaeta and Lois Ellis for turning their bakery into a television studio, and to head baker Horatio Garcia; to Al Abrahams, who never takes no for an answer, to Larry Feldman and Tom Eastman of Dynamic Cooking Systems for the beautiful ovens and cook top, and to Web master Jim Lewis for invaluable service all year long.

At St. Martin's Press, a debt of gratitude to Senior Editor Marian Lizzi for all her suggestions and enthusiasm for the manuscript. To Julie Mente, assistant editor; Jennifer Reeve, publicist with a vision; to Steve Snider, art director, for the beautiful cover, and to Robert Berkel, production editor, and Kate Nichols for the interior design of the book. Lastly, to our faithful readers and television audience, thank you for your continued good wishes.

He who has been in Italy can forget
all the other regions. Who has been in Heaven
does not desire the earth.

—NICOLAI GOGOL

Introduction

I T HAS ALWAYS SEEMED to me that when God needed a rest, He created Tuscany, and ever since then the world has claimed it as a prized vacation land. Toscana, Tuscany, has enjoyed international renown for a startling natural beauty that only Divine Providence could have conceived. It is Italy's fifth largest region, bordered on the west by the Ligurian Sea, Emilia Romagna to the north, the Marches and Umbria to the east, and Lazio to the southeast. Its major provinces are Florence, Arezzo, Carrara, Grosetto, Leghorn, Lucca, Pisa, Siena, and Pistoia.

Whenever I step into Tuscany, I find a region of sharp contrasts, a region known for landscapes so pristine that they seem too perfect to be true, and cities so choked with cars, Vespas, and people that it is almost impossible to move; a region of wheat fields so lush and high that they seem to form an expensive carpet, and neighborhoods so congested that relief must come in frequent trips to the countryside. It is a region whose museums are packed with much of the Western world's precious art. It is a region where the traditional way of life for the younger generation is being erased by runaway progress, and a region where ancient abbeys with their bell towers silhouetted against the skyline stirs in many a powerful urge to return to a simpler, more reflective life.

It is also a region that historically has been devoted to preserving its unique landscape, which in turn supports its culinary heritage, though today that heritage is in danger as more and more land is being bought by foreign interests using high-tech development to realize quick returns on their investments. As a consequence, much of Tuscany's natural food products are also in danger of disappearing.

This book is about the genuineness and simplicity of traditional Tuscan cooking. My hope is that in this book you will come to understand the foods of this region, often referred to as *cucina povera,* (poor cooking). This term does not mean to imply that the quality of the food is inferior or lacking in sophistication; instead it celebrates the region's basic food products, such as olives, wheat, cheeses, and wines. It is simple cooking that balks at pretense or fuss. Through cooking segments shot at various Tuscan locations, I met and cooked with some fascinating amateur and professional chefs who, through the dishes they created, made clear just what *cucina povera* means. Their honest, delicious, country-style dishes showcase the frugality as well as the genius of the Tuscan cook.

For many travelers, Tuscany *is* Italy, the land of Chianti wine and Michaelangelo. Ask people where they have been in Tuscany and invariably the answer is Florence, truly the art and architectural gem of the region, but not where you will find the whole picture of Tuscan life. For that you must peel away the outer layers of Tuscany, go beyond the tourist spots, and spend time with local families and businesspeople. This is how you'll come to understand what they value—family, religion, generosity of spirit, work ethic, pride, craftsmanship, oral traditions, and achievement. And, of course, food.

Tuscans look at food differently than we do; there is more reverence for it because they have a personal connection to the land, to the very way in which food is grown and harvested. Cooking means more to them than simply gathering ingredients together and calling it a meal. This was made very clear to me one day as I was purchasing some pears in a Cortona vegetable-and-fruit market. The woman who waited on me asked if I wanted hard or ripe pears, told me the story of growing and harvesting pears, asked how I was going to store them at home, and did not let me leave until she explained when was the best time to eat them! Now, *that* is connecting in a very meaningful way to food!

What is so special about Tuscan food? Simply put, it is simple ingredients simply prepared. Whimsy and pretense play no part in the Tuscan kitchen—no high-and-mighty sauces, no superimposed flavors, no artificial anything, and no tampering with what nature intended. These are the hallmarks of *cucina povera,* or as I like to think of it, country cooking.

In late Renaissance paintings and in old cooking manuscripts we can glimpse what Tuscans ate and have been eating for centuries, including olive oil, wine, cheese, beans, onions, and coarse breads. These foods are still the cornerstone of the basic Tuscan diet, as are vegetables (especially Swiss chard and black cabbage, called *cavolo nero*), grilled meats (especially pork, lamb, beef, and spicy home-made sausages), tripe, fish, wild boar, bread salads, grilled bread *(fettuna)*, and sweets such as *panforte* and *cantucci*.

Castello Banfi looms over the vineyards in the wine-producing area of Montalcino.

You can still find authentic preparations of these foods in Tuscan farm kitchens, or in home kitchens in quiet neighborhoods set among olive groves where the nearest "grocery store" is outside the back door in *un'orto* (the vegetable garden) in a plot or pot of earth. This is the Tuscany that I hoped to capture, and to set the scene I chose as my Tuscan home base a farm near Siena called Spannocchia (p. 1). The farm was the perfect place to tell the story of Tuscan food from the earth to the table. Every day on the farm, at every meal, I was treated to the freshest vegetables and breads made from wheat grown on the farm; I ate eggs from the hen house and meat from sheep, cows, and pigs allowed to roam free and eat natural feed. Of course, I was treated to the generosity and great spirit of my hosts, who personify Tuscany and its traditions.

Venturing beyond the farm, the search for real Tuscan food continued in small towns and villages, and in cities large and small, including Florence, Siena, and Pisa. In the markets and specialty shops I visited, foods straight off the farm are available for everyone. I've tried to capture the spirit of these exciting food spots, in addition to presenting their unique recipes.

By the time the filming was done, I had a better understanding of what *cucina povera* means. Tuscan food is about the careful and thoughtful ways foods are grown, and how they are preserved; it is about tomatoes strung for winter use, herbs dried into culinary bouquets, stale bread and bread crumbs magically turned into something new, milk transformed into cheese, grapes pressed into wine, and olives crushed for oil. Tuscan food is straightforward. I hope you will discover it for yourself in the pages of this book, then discover it again in your own kitchen.

Ciao Italia

IN TUSCANY

The Lord and Lady of Spannocchia

THROUGH A THICKET of woods lit by dappled sunlight, Spannocchia came into view. It is an old agricultural estate not too far from Siena and has a history that goes back over eight hundred years. A quick glance at my Italian dictionary told me that the word "spannocchiare" means to strip maize. It seems an appropriate name for a farm. It is also the name of the Spannocchi family, who resided here in the thirteenth century and operated the farm under the old *mezzadria* (the word means "half") system, which meant that peasant sharecroppers lived on the land in exchange for working it and providing half of the crop to the farm owners. Written documents show that in 1225 Zacaria dei Spannocchi gave a portion of the land to the monks of the nearby Santa Lucia monastery for the protection of the soul of his mother, donna Altigrada. The remains of the monastery and the early medieval fortress known as *Castiglione che Dio sol sa*, "the castle that only God knows," are still part of Spannocchia today.

The farm, encompassing over twelve hundred acres of vineyards, olive groves, fields, and forests, is now under the management and ownership of Francesca Cinelli Stratton, whose father bought the farm in the early twentieth century. Francesca married Randall Stratton, an architect, and together they are the modern lord and lady of the estate. Meeting them for the first time and seeing the expanse that is in their care made me marvel at their dedication in striving to keep Spannocchia a working farm dedicated to mixing old traditional methods with modern-day organic ones.

It is clear to me that Francesca, whose grandfather was born near Florence and who oversees the household, the farmhands, and the visitors who come to Spannocchia, has the resolve and enthusiasm to carry on her family's legacy, and that Randall, who is soft-spoken and cautious, is eager to preserve the "living museum" aspect of the farm with its magnificent stone sixteenth-century villa, twelfth-century castle tower, and numerous outbuildings.

Most of the farm laborers are young, coming from all over the States. In exchange for room and board they work on the farm, clearing forests, planting crops, and fixing buildings. They preserve old ways while learning from the past.

On my arrival Randall was kind enough to give me a walking tour of the estate, which would be my home for the duration of our filming in Tuscany for *Ciao Italia*. I would be staying in room number three in the villa for three weeks, and I was kindly informed that a friendly ghost by the name of Pia inhabits room number five. There are no locks on any of the doors.

The grounds around the sand-colored villa are spectacular, with magnificent cypress trees lining the main stone road *(strada bianca)*; they stand erect like missles bound for a Wedgwood-blue sky. The many private roads and trails tantalize the visitor to take a look at gigantic holm oak, chestnut, and pine trees. Deep into the forest wild boar are foraging, sharing space with rare breeds of animals including the *Cintasenese* pigs, with their wide belt-like center white stripe, and *Colvana* cows. There is also a gentle breed of sheep called *Pomarancina* that comes from nearby Pisa. The farm is committed to preserving these endangered species.

In *il campo* (the field) one can find plantings of ancient wheat strains such as *farro,* a cousin of emmer, as well as barley and fava beans for the pigs. The whole idea is to be self-sufficient, but, as Randall cautioned me, that idea had not yet sunk in with Francesca, who still thinks it necessary to travel to the nearby *supermercato* to shop for groceries.

Walking over to the vegetable garden I noticed a small chapel almost covered by the surrounding foliage; Randall told me that it is still used by visiting clergy to say Mass. This is yet another sign of how life was lived hundreds of years ago, when wealthy families could summon the clergy to say Mass in their own private chapel.

Over by the vegetable garden the sun beat down on interns in tattered straw hats as they harvested beans, tomatoes, herbs, and cardoons to be used in the kitchen that night as part of the evening meal. Tergo Trapassi, who oversees the vegetable gardens and vine-yards, is an elderly gentleman. He began farming when he was only a boy of twelve, and he now plays the part of a wizened farmer perfectly with an encyclopedic mind full of gardening tricks and all kinds of advice at the ready. Just as we began to talk about Tergo's favorite tomatoes, Francesca invited me to join her and the farmhands for lunch.

The kitchen is located in the villa right next to the rustic dining room with its long wooden tables set with sturdy dishes and ready to receive the

Randall Stratton shows me around the centuries-old farm known as Spannocchia.

farmhands, who sit on no-nonsense chairs. Lunch is right off the farm: bean salads, olives, greens dressed with olive oil, homemade bread, slabs of pecorino cheese, and ham. The food is simple, plentiful, and delicious. Francesca and Randall told me about their vision for Spannocchia and their goal of maintaining the quality of life there for future generations. It is a tall order when one considers the many projects going on there, the ongoing architectural preservation, the management and restoration of the woodlands, and, of course, maintaining the organic farm.

After lunch I was led down a long corridor to my room. On the way we stopped in the library, which houses voluminous documentation about Spannocchia's beginnings and what kind of crops were grown and sold there. On the ceiling of the library is the Spannocchia coat of arms, depicting *pannòcchia*, corn cobs. The library holds a lot of secrets about Spannocchia, and I made a mental note to come back when time permitted.

My room was sparse, like a farm room should be; there was a bed and dresser, and a bathroom the size of a small closet. On the walls were old photos of Francesca's relatives who once lived at Spannocchia. She was there, too, a beauty with brownish blond hair. I threw open the shutters and the commanding view of olive trees, fields, and old buildings more than made up for the sparseness of my room. The sun was beginning to fade at the edge of the landscape and Francesca and Randall suggested that I rest. At last I could give in to jet lag. I saw them out the door, they are perfectly suited to being the lord and lady of the estate and they made me feel right at home.

Lying down, I pulled the covers over me. Sleep came easily, even knowing that, two doors away, Pia might visit me at any time.

The Mindful Gardener

Carciofi in Umido (Braised Artichokes)

Crema di Porri (Creamed Leeks)

Porrata (Leek Tart)

I HAD A DATE on the farm at Spannocchia with Tergo Trapassi, the head vegetable gardener. We would spend time together on that glorious spring day visiting the produce gardens that are his responsibility to oversee. As I walked to our meeting point I thought about my own vegetable garden in New Hampshire, and how even then, in mid-May, it was still too cold to put much of anything in the ground. But at Spannocchia the harvest of spring vegetables was under way. Just a tinge of jealousy moved through me as I swung open the garden gate.

Tergo, an older man with a sweet face, was waiting for me near the cardoon patch. He was dressed in a plaid shirt and wool hat. He looked like the perfect gardener, and I knew he must be when I shook his weathered, sandpaper hands, a telltale sign that he not only oversees but works the land as well. For close to half a century, starting when he was twelve, he has been wedded to the earth, so his wisdom about growing vegetables comes not from books but from experience. There was so much I wanted to ask him, so I started with what I thought our television audience would like to know. We start with tomatoes. According to Tergo, there are four kinds of tomatoes worth his time: *mele* (apple), *San Marzano,* the favorite plum variety to make tomato sauce ragu, *cuore* (heart), so named for its juiciness and size, and *bombolini* (little bombs), small, yellow cherry tomatoes. I pressed him further. *Which tomatoes are best for salads?* Tergo reinforced what I have long known: Italians like greenish plum tomatoes a bit on the hard side for salad because they hold up better, while ripe ones are pulpier and better for making sauces.

In the artichoke patch with Tergo Trapassi.

We walked along the path of the garden with the camera crew trailing us. "See that wild mint?" he asked. I plucked a sprig of *mentuccia*, but Tergo quickly corrected me and said that, here, mint is called *mentrasta*. He likes to make a drink with it when he is under the weather.

Next were cardoons (*cardi*), a thistlelike plant that in one part of the garden was taller than me. I have always shied away from cooking them because they take so much time to prepare. Their sturdy stalks need to be peeled before boiling; I see them as a vegetable that will soon be forgotten on the younger Italian generation's table. Rarely do I see cardoons offered batter-fried, as was the custom at home when my grandmother gathered wild ones from along the roadsides.

One of my favorite vegetables, leeks, was growing there as well. It was exciting to see such vigorous and tall ones, and I complimented Tergo on them. He shook a weak finger at them and told me they are not his favorite, and his wife will not cook them. "Oh, but I should make you my leek tart," I told him, "*that I know you would like.*"

Tergo guided me to his favorite artichoke patch, truly an impressive sight. He showed me the two varieties that grow there—one is red with spines and the other—his favorite, called *morello*—is green without spines. With a small pocket knife he snapped one off the stalk, whittled away the stem like a wood carver, and cut it into slices. "Try it, it is tender without cooking," he beamed. Tergo likes the slices just drizzled with olive oil and salt. Larger artichokes are prepared filled with bread crumbs, egg, ground pork, garlic, salt and pepper, and cooked in a skillet with olive oil.

There isn't much that Tergo does not know about plants. He grows a lot of fava beans. Some will be eaten raw with pecorino cheese, others will be dried and ground into flour, and some stored as feed for the pigs. In the *campo* (field) the wheat shafts stood tall, blowing in unison in the wind. Tergo grows *farro*, an ancient wheat grain packed with a lot of nutrients. It is harvested and sold in the farm store. I told him that Americans are just discovering *farro* and how to cook it, which brought out a deep belly laugh from him, since he has been eating it all his life.

What is a Tuscan garden without herbs? Tergo motioned me to the parsley, basil, sage, rosemary, and thyme growing in a sunny spot near the garden wall. He bent down to get me a bouquet of those, since he knew I would be cooking later in the farm kitchen. Although sage *(salvia)* seems to be most Tuscans' favorite herb, he is partial to thyme because he likes cheese. I missed the significance of what he was saying until he quoted an old Tuscan proverb: "If you want good cheese and a good time, send your sheep to graze on thyme." And since he always has parsley *(prezzemolo)* growing in the garden he is proud of another wise saying: "He (or she) is like parsley," a compliment meaning you can always count on someone being there for you, just as he can always count on having a ready supply of parsley.

Just listening to Tergo gave me a new appreciation for my own garden. His wise words and self-taught knowledge of the garden humbled me. I asked Tergo why he loves gardening so much after all these years. "The garden is a metaphor for life; it teaches me patience," he said. "It talks to me all year long, telling me to be observant, to anticipate, and be faithful to its needs. Everything that happens in the garden depends on me. If I work hard, it rewards me with good food coming from my own hands. What else do I need?" I could only answer "nothing" to this mindful gardener.

Carciofi in Umido
Braised Artichokes

SERVES 4

2 large artichokes

Juice of 1 lemon

2 tablespoons unsalted butter

2 tablespoons extra-virgin olive oil

2 cloves garlic, minced

2 tablespoons minced parsley

½ teaspoon fine sea salt

2 tablespoons half-and-half or cream

¼ cup dry white wine

I scribbled this recipe for braised artichokes on a piece of paper and gave it to Tergo to have his wife make for him at home.

Wash and dry the artichokes. Roll them on the countertop under your hands to loosen the leaves. Cut off the stems and remove the tough outer leaves at the base—I usually remove two or three layers. Cut ¼ inch off the tip of each artichoke and trim the prickly thorns on the remaining leaves. Open the center of each artichoke and remove the hairy choke with a spoon. This is the part that Tergo does not have to deal with, since his artichokes are chokeless.

Cut the artichokes in half, then in quarters. Place the quarters in a bowl with the lemon juice; this helps prevent the browning of the surface of the pieces. Let them soak for about 20 minutes, then drain them and dry well.

In a small, heavy Dutch oven–type pan, heat the butter and oil. Stir in the garlic and cook until it begins to soften. Stir in the parsley and continue to cook over low heat for 3 minutes. Add the artichoke quarters, coating them well in the seasonings. Sprinkle the salt over the quarters and continue to cook for 5 minutes. Add the half-and-half or cream and half the wine and cook covered for 15 minutes. Add the remaining wine and cook until a knife is easily inserted into the leaves and heart. Serve with some of the pan juices.

Crema di Porri
Creamed Leeks

SERVES 6 TO 8

Leeks (porri), *part of the onion family, were favorites of the ancient Romans and are still much appreciated today in Tuscan cooking. In this preparation the objective is to achieve a thick, smooth, and creamy consistency.*

Cut the leeks in half lengthwise. Wash them well to remove any dirt and cut them into thin slices.

Melt the butter in a 3-quart saucepan, add the leeks, and cook them very slowly until they soften, about 5 minutes. Stir in the flour and cook 1 minute. Slowly pour in the broth and stir to keep the mixture smooth. Cook over medium heat until the mixture is soft and pureed-looking but not too thick, about 10 minutes.

Remove the pan from the flame. Stir in the thyme, salt, and pepper. Transfer the mixture to a serving dish and sprinkle with the cheese.

Serve the leeks in small bowls accompanied with slices of toasted bread.

2 pounds leeks, trimmed and dark green leaves removed

2 tablespoons unsalted butter

2 tablespoons flour

4 cups hot chicken broth

2 tablespoons finely minced thyme

Fine sea salt to taste

Coarse white pepper to taste

Grated Parmigiano-Reggiano cheese for sprinkling on top

Porrata
Leek Tart

SERVES 6 TO 8

DOUGH

1 teaspoon active
dry yeast

1 cup warm water
(110°F)

2 tablespoons extra-virgin
olive oil

1 large egg

½ teaspoon fine sea salt

3¾ to 4 cups unbleached
all-purpose flour

FILLING

2 pounds leeks,
dark green stem tops
and roots removed

4 tablespoons extra-virgin
olive oil

½ cup dry white wine
such as Pinot Grigio

2 large eggs

½ teaspoon salt

Coarse white pepper
to taste

¼ pound prosciutto,
mortadella, or
cooked ham, diced

*T*he name porrata *has a nice ring to it. It means "leek tart," and was originally made to commemorate religious functions staged in San Lorenzo during the month of August. This tart is considered to be an antipasto, but I like to make it as a main course. It may seem like an overabundance of leeks are called for—two pounds—but it makes the perfect amount of filling for a 10½-inch tart shell pan. The yeast dough is easily made in a food processor or by hand, and you can make the filling two days ahead of time.*

Dissolve the yeast in ¼ cup of the warm water and allow it to get chalky looking, about 5 minutes. Transfer the yeast mixture to the bowl of a food processor, or pour it into a large bowl if doing this by hand. Pour in the remaining water, the olive oil, and egg and combine well.

Add the salt and 3½ cups of the flour. Pulse to mix the ingredients, or mix by hand. Stir in the remaining flour a little at a time until a smooth ball of dough moves away from the side of the processor or the bowl. The dough should feel soft and smooth and not be sticking to your hands. You may or may not need all the flour.

If you used the food processor, transfer the dough to a bowl and cover the bowl tightly with plastic wrap. Otherwise, use the same bowl you worked the dough in by hand. Allow the dough to double in size (about 2 hours) in a warm spot.

Meanwhile, make the filling:

Wash the leeks well, as they can be very sandy. Dry them with paper towels and with a knife cut them lengthwise and then widthwise into ¼-inch-thick slices.

In a large sauté pan heat the olive oil, add the leeks and cook them covered over low heat stirring frequently until they soften, about 5 minutes. Uncover the pan, raise the heat to high, pour in the wine and allow most of it to evaporate. Cover the pan, reduce the heat to low and cook until the leeks are very soft and creamy looking.

Transfer the leeks to a bowl, and when they are cool stir in the eggs, salt, and a good grinding of the pepper. Cover and refrigerate the mixture until ready to fill the tart shell. This step can be done two days ahead of time.

Lightly oil a 10½-inch tart shell with a removable bottom and set aside.

Preheat the oven to 375°F.

Punch down the dough with your fists and divide it in half; roll one half into a 13-inch round and fit it into the tart shell. Cut off the excess dough with a scissors. Scatter the prosciutto or other meats in the base of the shell, then spread the leek mixture over the top. Roll out the second half of the dough to fit the top of the tart pan, allowing for the dough to overhang the pan. Roll over the top of the crust gently with a rolling pin to trim and seal the edges.

Reroll the scraps and use a cookie cutter to make designs for the top of the tart if you wish, or simply make a couple of small rolls to bake along with the tart.

Bake the tart for 35 to 40 minutes, or until the top is nicely browned.

Allow the tart to cool before removing the side rim. Cut into wedges and serve warm or at room temperature.

The Roman emperor Nero, who loved to sing, ate leeks every day to keep his throat clear. He believed leeks kept his vocal chords in good condition.

When Tuscan Women Cook

Cinghiale al Vino
(Wild Boar Stew in Wine)

Pappardelle (Wide Homemade Noodles)

Petti di Pollo al Vino Bianco
(Chicken Breasts in White Wine)

Salame Dolce (Chocolate Cookies)

G RAZIELLA CAPANNI and Gaetana Caglione are not afraid of hard work; they've been accustomed to it from a young age. From early in the morning when the first rooster crows, to when the last dish is washed after the evening meal, they are all business and concentration in the farm kitchen of Spannocchia. It is their job as cooks to turn out simple Tuscan fare for the owner and his family, the many farmhands, and the visitors who stay on the farm. Graziella, shy with a sweet baby face, was born near Spannocchia and is older than Gaetana, who comes from the hills around Naples and has the rosiest cheeks that I have ever seen. Both learned how to make pasta when they were young girls. For their generation, it was considered a right of passage, though sadly this is no longer the case in Italy.

What they cook is just as important as *how* they cook. The meals are decided by what is growing on the farm, and, like the good cooks they are, they make use of everything. I let them know that they would be on television that day, and I couldn't tell if their semismiles were out of nervousness or if they were just trying to be demure. Graziella was cleaning celery, onions, carrots, and parsley to be minced into a *battuto* in the large stone sink at one end of the compact kitchen. Gaetana was preparing to make a ragù. The plan was to cook *cinghiale*, wild boar, in a wine sauce, a typical Tuscan dish, but Graziella and Gaetana looked a bit puzzled when I went over the plan and they asked me if I knew how to make it. Together we washed and dried the boar meat, which was butchered during the winter months and frozen. I showed them how I season it with salt,

Gaetana and Graziella smile after the taping segment on wild boar.

pepper, and flour while Graziella added the *battuto* and aromatic herbs to a huge pot. As soon as the vegetables hit the hot oil the room was cloaked in the authentic cooking smells of Tuscany. We added the meat chunks and browned them well, then poured in wine made on the farm from Sangiovese grapes. We covered the pot and let it go while we turned our attention to making the tagliatelle, ribbon-shaped noodles that would be served with the ragù sauce.

On a large, worn, marble table, Graziella heaped a Mount Everest of flour, plunged her fist into it to make the classic hole in the center, and cracked in thirty eggs. Next she put on rubber gloves, which puzzled me. I didn't want to seem rude, but I had never seen anyone make pasta with rubber gloves on. I could not resist asking her why, and she told me that it is a way to keep her hands clean when she is preparing so many different foods at the same time, which immediately made a lot of sense.

Together we kneaded the mass of dough into a huge golden ball, then cut and rolled pieces of it through a hand-crank pasta machine before cutting it into strands. It would be plenty to serve the thirty guests that were expected.

For Graziella and Gaetana the day was very intense. They would also prepare and cook spinach for the night's vegetable offering, peel fava beans to be served raw with pecorino cheese, fry sage leaves to be served with an anchovy paste, and wrap dried prunes in prosciutto for an antipasto. They had to think of dessert, too, and there is where the cleverness of those cooks really shined. A tin full of cookie crumbs, mixed with nuts, cocoa, and sugar and moistened with wine, became something grand . . . *salame dolce* (sweet salami) (p. 25), a slice-and-eat, no-bake confection that looks a lot like a slice of salami.

Another successful meal at the hands of these two accomplished, self-taught cooks had everyone in the dining room applauding. Graziella and Gaetana cheerfully waved good-bye and headed out the door to their own homes to begin the process again for their own families. The next day, when the rooster sounded his daylight call, they would stand for long hours again in the kitchen, using their wits and cooking from instinct, and a sense of pride, while whetting the appetites of all who would be privileged to enjoy true Tuscan country cooking, *cucina povera,* at its very best.

Cinghiale al Vino
Wild Boar Stew in Wine

SERVES 10 TO 12

4 celery stalks with tops, cut into quarters

5 small onions, peeled and quartered

6 medium carrots, quartered

3 large garlic cloves, peeled

1 cup parsley leaves

½ cup sage leaves

⅓ cup rosemary needles

½ cup extra-virgin olive oil

3 pounds boar or beef stew meat cut into 1-inch pieces

1 cup flour

2 teaspoons fine sea salt

1 teaspoon ground black pepper

3½–4 cups Chianti wine

Wild boar is synonymous with Tuscany. Many places selling the meat have a boar's head displayed somewhere in the shop or out by the doorway. The best way to cook it is in a stew with aromatic vegetables and a good red wine. This is the dish I made for the farmhands at Spannocchia, with some help from Graziella and Gaetana, who prepared the battuto, *the aromatic vegetables that would be reduced to a fine mince and used to flavor the stew. The recipe is enough for a crowd or for freezing for later use. Stew beef can be substituted for the boar.*

To make quick work of the *battuto,* put the celery, onions, carrots, and garlic in a food processor and pulse until the ingredients look coarse. Add the parsley, sage, and rosemary needles and continue to process until there is a fine mixture. Or use a chef's knife and mince all the ingredients.

In a large soup pot heat the olive oil; when it begins to shimmer, lower the heat to medium and stir in the *battuto* ingredients. Cook the mixture, stirring occasionally until the vegetables are wilted.

Dry the meat pieces with paper towels. In a large bag combine the flour, salt, and pepper. Add the meat pieces, close the bag at the top and shake it vigorously to coat the meat in the flour mixture. Shake off the excess flour and place the meat on a dish.

Remove the wilted vegetables to a dish and set aside. If the pan seems dry pour in 2 tablespoons of olive oil. Raise the heat to medium-high and brown the meat, in batches if necessary, until it is nicely browned. Raise the heat to high and pour in the wine. Allow it to come to a boil, then reduce the heat to low and stir in the reserved vegetables.

Add additional wine to just cover the meat, if necessary. Cover the pot and allow the stew to cook for about 2 hours or until the meat is fork tender.

Correct the seasoning by adding additional salt and pepper if necessary.

Serve the stew hot.

Pappardelle
Wide Homemade Noodles

MAKES ABOUT 1¼ POUNDS
(ENOUGH TO SERVE 6 TO 8)

3 cups unbleached
all-purpose flour

4 large eggs

¼ teaspoon fine sea salt

*G*raziella and Gaetana make just about every type of fresh pasta, *including* pappardelle, *wide noodles so light in texture that it is conceivable that too many could be consumed with no difficulty at all. That is not surprising, given that the word* pappardelle *means to gorge. They are often served with wild hare, but your favorite pasta sauce works well, too.*

Pour the flour in a heap on a work surface and use your hands to make a hole, or *fontana*, as Italian cooks call it, in the middle of the flour. Crack the eggs into the center, add the salt, and use your hands to whip them around to break them up as you blend it all together.

Begin bringing some of the flour from the inside of the flour wall into the center, mixing it with the eggs. Continue this way until enough of the flour has been added to make a rough-looking ball of dough. Push the excess flour aside, and knead the dough until it becomes smooth with no bumpy spots, and it is not sticking to your hands. The dough should feel soft; adding too much flour will produce a dry dough.

Now form the dough into a ball and put it on a lightly floured surface. Put a bowl over the top of it and allow it to rest for about 30 minutes. This will help to relax the gluten in the dough and make it easier to roll out.

Cut the dough into thirds and work with one piece at a time; keep the remaining pieces covered so they do not dry out.

Use a rolling pin to roll the pieces out on a lightly floured surface into a 14 × 16-inch rectangle that is about ¹⁄₁₆ inch thick. I use a pastry wheel to cut ½-inch wide strips to make the *pappardelle*.

After cutting them, put them on clean towels to dry or to hold until ready to cook them.

To cook *pappardelle* or any other fresh pasta, start with a large pot of boiling water, at least 4 to 6 quarts. Add 1 tablespoon of salt to the boiling water for every pound of pasta. Add the *pappardelle*. Remember that fresh pasta cooks in no time at all, and should remain *al dente*, meaning it should be firm, not mushy, but cooked through. Cook the *pappardelle* for no longer than 3 to 4 minutes. Drain it in a colander and toss it with your favorite sauce.

Petti di Pollo al Vino Bianco
Chicken Breasts in White Wine

SERVES 4

3 pounds whole chicken breasts, boned

½ cup flour for dredging

¼ teaspoon fine sea salt

¼ teaspoon black pepper

½ cup extra-virgin olive oil

4 tablespoons unsalted butter, cut into pieces

6 cloves garlic, cut into thin slices

8 large sage leaves

1 cup dry white wine

I was truly spoiled by the food served at Spannocchia. Everything was, to use a cliché, "right off the farm," so it was the freshest it could be. I fell in love with this delicious and easy-to-prepare chicken dish flavored with wine and sage that Graziella and Gaetana prepared one night for dinner. Of course, the quality of the chicken is critical. On the farm, chickens are fed natural grains and are allowed to wander. So when you try this recipe, use free-range chicken if possible; you will definitely taste a difference.

Preheat the oven to 400°F.

Cut the chicken breasts horizontally into 2-inch-wide strips.

Mix flour, salt, and pepper on a plate. Dredge each chicken strip in the flour mixture and set aside on a plate.

Pour the olive oil into a large baking pan, or use two smaller ones to hold the pieces in a single layer, and divide the ingredients between the two pans. Scatter the butter, garlic, and sage leaves over the oil. Lay the chicken strips on top. Bake until browned, turning the strips once.

Halfway through the cooking, add the wine and continue to bake for another 15 to 20 minutes, until the wine has cooked down and forms a sauce. Serve the chicken with some of the juices poured over the strips.

NOTE: When dealing with raw chicken or meat, prepare everything you need for the recipe before you begin to cook, saving the chicken as the last to be prepped. Have paper towels handy so you do not contaminate the kitchen area as you work. After the dish is ready, wash your hands in hot soapy water and disinfect the sink and counter areas where you have worked.

Salame Dolce
Chocolate Cookies

SERVES 20 TO 25

Graziella and Gaetana usually make the most of what is in season in the Spannocchia vegetable garden and larder, and they are equally as enterprising when it comes to creating something sweet for hungry farmhands. They can take a box of plain cookies and turn it in no time at all into a classic Tuscan no-bake cookie they call salame dolce, *or sweet salami. These refrigerated logs have the appearance of salami when sliced. They are delicious and keep well in the refrigerator for weeks—but I can guarantee you that they will not last longer than a day or two.*

Reduce the cookies to fine crumbs in a food processor or in a paper bag, crushing them with a rolling pin. Transfer the crumbs to a large mixing bowl and mix in the cocoas, sugar, and almonds.

Mix the butter with the egg yolks and stir into the cocoa mixture.

Mix everything well with your hands, adding a tablespoon at a time of Vin Santo or brandy until the ingredients are wet enough to hold together without crumbling.

Cut a piece of plastic wrap at least 16 inches long. Spread the mixture along the middle of the wrap. Fold up one long side to start forming a 12 or 14 × 2-inch salami-shaped log. Bring the opposite side of the wrap up and compress the mixture into a log shape. Twist the ends to seal the log and reshape it with your hands so it is even-looking. Refrigerate several hours.

Spread a thick layer of sugar over a work surface. Unwrap the *salame* and roll it in the sugar to coat it well.

Rewrap the log and refrigerate it for several hours to make it easier to slice.

To serve, cut the log into ¼ to ½-inch slices.

1 pound plain tea cookies, such as Lorna Doone or Danish butter cookies

¼ cup Dutch-process cocoa (Droste)

½ cup sweet cocoa (Ghirardelli)

¾ cup unsweetened baking cocoa (Hershey's)

1¼ cups sugar

⅔ cup slivered almonds

½ cup plus 2 tablespoons unsalted butter, melted and cooled

3 extra large egg yolks, slightly beaten

3 to 5 tablespoons Vin Santo or brandy, as needed

Granulated, coarse, or turbinado sugar

NOTE: To get a perfect cylindrical shape, try using an old waxed-paper or aluminum-foil cardboard (inner) tube and place the plastic-wrapped log inside. Roll it around on the counter to conform to the tube's shape. Refrigerate and slice as directed.

My Big, Fat Tuscan Pizza(s)

Schiacciata alle Olive (Olive Pizza)

Pasta per Pizza (Basic Pizza Dough)

DO YOU REMEMBER the old Prince Spaghetti television commercials showing a little boy named Anthony answering his mother's long, piercing call to come in for dinner? The message was that every Wednesday was Prince Spaghetti day. Well I felt a little like Anthony while living on the farm estate at Spannocchia. There, every other Wednesday was pizza day, when all the farmhands, managers, and guests of the estate eagerly looked forward to getting together and eating pizza at long wooden tables set up outdoors.

It seems the tradition was started by some of the American interns who took it upon themselves to fire up the outdoor wood-burning oven and make and serve an array of pizzas sporting traditional toppings, from fresh tomatoes and mozzarella cheese to not-so-traditional, bizarre toppings of canned pineapple chunks and sliced hot dogs!

The art of making pizza is not native to Tuscany—for that you must go to Naples, the real home of authentically prepared pizza—nevertheless, pizza is a ubiquitous food found in many guises and under many local names all over Italy, and Spannocchia is no exception.

Getting ready for this pizza party was not easy. The fire needed to be started early in the afternoon and had to blaze until the coals turned hellish red—then they were raked to the sides of the oven and the floor of the oven was brushed clean, ready to receive the dough.

Watching this process gave me a new appreciation for the way things are done on the farm. The dough was made from wheat grown there; the fire was

Pizza night at Spannocchia.

started with clippings from pruned grape vines and olive trees, and the toppings—the cheese, vegetables, and herbs—were grown on the farm, too. The small feast was definitely a grassroots event.

The fun began when the pizza dough was brought from the kitchen on long wooden peels, topped with a variety of ingredients, and slid onto the oven floor, where they take only a few minutes to cook. One by one, like precision clockwork, they were fished out of the oven onto the peels, the outer edges of the dough charred just enough to remind us that this is the real way to bake pizza, and the middle still soft, just the way it should be. They were immediately brought to the table accompanied by the oohs and aahs of the fork-ready diners. The passage of pizza along the table route began. And of course you had to try each one! Thin as parchment paper and emitting delicious smells, they were devoured along with glasses of homemade wine.

I had to hand it to the *pizzaiolo* on duty that day for imagination run wild. There was Gorgonzola-and-pear pizza, classic *Margherita* pizza, eggplant, zucchini, and leek pizza, caramelized onion and walnut pizza, artichoke pizza, sausage pizza, potato-and-olive pizza, and . . . I stopped counting after the ninth one. As I enjoyed them with the rest of the guests I thought about the uniqueness of our simple but delightful meal—but could not bring myself to indulge in pineapple and hot dog pizza. I do have my standards!

Schiacciata alle Olive
Olive Pizza

SERVES 8 TO 10 AS AN ANTIPASTO

S chiacciata *means squashed or flattened bread, as in the variety of* schiacciate *one can find in bars or* pasticerrie *(pastry shops) in Tuscany. To me it is just another word for pizza, a flat pie. Call it* schiacciata *or pizza, Tuscans flavor theirs with herbs, olives, cheese, cured meats, and vegetables. This pizza is light in texture, more cake-like due to the egg in the dough, and is made in a jelly roll pan and cut into squares, which makes a great antipasto for a party.*

Dissolve the yeast and sugar in the water in a large bowl. Allow it to stand and get muddy-looking, about 10 minutes. Stir in 1 table-spoon of the olive oil and the egg and beat with a whisk to blend.

Stir in 3 cups of the flour and mix with your hands until a dough starts to form. Add additional flour and the salt until you have a soft dough that is not sticking to your hands.

Grease a large bowl with 1 teaspoon of the remaining olive oil, wipe the dough in the oil, turning it several times, and cover the bowl tightly with plastic wrap. Let it rise in a place that is not too warm (75°F is ideal) until doubled in size, about 1 hour.

Preheat the oven to 425°F.

Grease a 17 × 11-inch jelly roll or other similar pan with the remaining 1 tablespoon of olive oil. Set the pan aside.

Punch the dough down on a floured surface and roll it out with a rolling pin to fit the pan. Fit the dough into the pan, bringing the edges up the sides.

Spread the tomato sauce evenly over the dough. Sprinkle the oregano over the sauce. Evenly space the olives, cut side down over the sauce. Sprinkle the cheese evenly over the olives. Bake for 35 to 40 minutes, or until the bottom crust is nicely browned. Cool slightly for even cutting. Serve warm or at room temperature.

DOUGH

1 teaspoon dried yeast

1 teaspoon sugar

1½ cups warm water (110°F)

2 tablespoons plus 1 teaspoon extra-virgin olive oil

1 large egg at room temperature

4 to 4½ cups unbleached all-purpose flour

½ teaspoon fine sea salt

TOPPING

2 cups prepared tomato sauce

1 tablespoon dried oregano

½ cup oil-cured black olives, pitted and halved

⅔ cup grated pecorino cheese

Pasta per Pizza
Basic Pizza Dough

MAKES 1 POUND, 14 OUNCES OF DOUGH

1 package dry yeast

1¾ cups warm water
(110°F)

1 tablespoon extra-virgin
olive oil

4 to 4½ cups unbleached
all-purpose flour

2 teaspoons fine sea salt

This is my standard recipe for pizza dough, but it can be used to make fried dough, calzones, or a loaf of bread. Use filtered water if possible, because tap water sometimes has an off taste and can affect the taste of the dough.

Dissolve the yeast in ½ cup of the water in a large bowl and allow it to stand for about 10 minutes to proof or get chalky and bubbly. Pour in the remaining water and olive oil. Begin adding the flour to the yeast mixture 1 cup at a time, mixing it well with your hands, or use a stand mixer or a food processor to make the dough. Add the salt with the third cup of flour. Add just enough flour so that the dough comes together in a shaggy mass. Turn it out onto a lightly floured surface and knead it until it is smooth.

Grease a large bowl with 1 teaspoon of olive oil and coat the dough in the oil in the bowl. Cover the bowl tightly with plastic wrap and allow it to rise until doubled in size, about 1 hour.

Punch down the dough and divide it in half. Roll each half out to fit a standard-size pizza pan. Cover the dough with the toppings of your choice.

To bake, preheat the oven to 375°F, or, if you are using a baking stone, preheat the oven 30 minutes prior to baking at 450°F and use oven peels lined with either cornmeal or parchment paper.

Bake the pizza until the bottom crust is nicely browned.

The Little Church with the Blue Door

When we're filming on location, it's a rare treat to get a day off. So I was delighted one day when my executive producer, Paul Lally, told me I was free to explore Tuscany without any taping schedule. With photographer Bill Truslow and our senior culinary supervisor, Donna Petti-Soares, we set out for adventure. A sign announcing the town of Lucignano caught my attention, so we made it our destination for an espresso and some much-needed relaxation. Lucignano, situated on a hillside lush with olive and cypress trees, is not far from Arezzo and still maintains its medieval look.

It was market day when we arrived and things were winding down as the vendors were folding up their movable shops and heading out of town. Luckily, a bar was still open, and we ordered espresso and sat in the warm sun before deciding to split up to wander around on our own. Travelers come to Lucignano to marvel at the unusual elliptical layout of the town streets, four concentric circles that literally have *you* walking in circles! While taking scenic photographs, following the circular streets, I wound up at the dear little church of San Francesco, built in the thirteenth century. It was the robin's-egg-blue door that attracted me to it. This compact church sits tucked into a small space near the Palazzo Comunale. I love it for its scale. At first glance it does not seem like a church at all, but a dollhouse that any child would want to play in. The Roman façade is striking in its stark, clean lines, with bands of horizontal gray-and-white marble wrapped around it, giving it a zebra effect. And the Gothic arch over the doorway seems to balance the simple rosetta window above it at its peak. It said to me: *Come and pray.* But to do so one must summon the caretaker who lives next door. I rang the bell and an elderly woman in a flowered apron appeared. I asked if I could see the church and she handed me a huge iron key. "Bring it back when you are done praying," she told me. I put the key, which seemed almost as big as the church itself, into the rusty keyhole and let myself in. I felt like magic was about to happen. Once I passed through the door, serenity overtook me. Inside, the church was even simpler than its exterior but in the nave, badly damaged and fragmented frescoes told a rich story of the life of Saint Francis, the itinerant preacher from Assisi who founded the Franciscan order and walked his way across Italy bringing the message of hope and peace to anyone who would listen, even birds and wolves.

The frescoes still maintain patches of their vivid colors of rose, green, gold, and that enchanting robin's-egg blue, and are the work of artists Bartolo di Fredi, and Taddeo di Bartolo. Their depictions show Saint Francis with the stigmata (the wounds of Christ), praying in the desert, preaching with his brother friars, and talking to ferocious and gentle animals all harmoniously drinking out of the same fountain, a vivid metaphor for compatibility and living in peace. It seemed that I was inside for just moments, but a glance at my watch told me that it had been almost an hour! I took one last look, closed and locked the door, and returned the key. I felt fortunate on a day given as a gift of leisure, to have entered this peaceful space hidden inside the little church with the blue door.

To Eat Like a Florentine

Bistecca alla Fiorentina
(Grilled T-Bone Steak)

Pesto (Basil Sauce)

Pollo al Mattone
(Chicken Cooked Under Bricks)

Salsa di Pomodori Ciliegini e Pesto
(Cherry Tomato–Pesto Sauce)

Tuttoinsieme (Mixed Vegetables)

THE LITTLE *BORGO* of Bignola is quaint, cozy, colorful, and quiet. Just seven miles from the frenzy of Florence, it is a DOGCO (denomination of guaranteed controlled origin) Chianti wine–producing area, a picture-perfect silent valley with seemingly endless vineyard plantings and wispy olive trees squeezed on hillsides here and there. This is home for our friends Adalgisa and Eduardo Catamario and about thirty other residents. Their stone house, like the others in the neighborhood, is embellished with welcoming pots of colorful geraniums and trailing purple bouganvilla.

Neither Adalgisa—"Gi" as she is called—nor Eduardo are Tuscans; she was born to the south, in Lecce in the region of Puglia, and he was born in Naples. But they have forged a life in Tuscany that suits their lifestyle. Gi works in the travel industry, and with her dark hair and piercing blue eyes she could pass for a model. Eduardo is muscular, with a thick head of hair, a jovial smile, and a strong voice that is very lyrical. He is a classical guitarist who travels the world performing in concert. Because he needs to concentrate when composing music they live in Bignola, where there is scant noise or disruption to interrupt his work.

Filming them at home—Gi in the kitchen preparing typical Florentine fare and Eduardo performing on the guitar—was my goal the day that we arrived. I wanted it to be a comfortable behind-the-scenes look at Italian life as it is lived, not according to Hollywood, but according to them.

We were welcomed warmly and ushered into the neat-as-a-pin kitchen. Gi

Gi is ready to serve the tagliata, bistecca *with lettuce greens.*

had been preparing the fireplace grill all morning for cooking the classic *bistecca alla fiorentina*—or to be more mundane about it, a thick T-bone steak. She was busy using a bellows to fan the flames, but it was so small I wondered how she would ever get the coals hot enough. The huge steak, more than an inch thick, was deep red in color and made a statement on the plate. It comes from a special breed of cow called *Chianina* for which Tuscany is famous, and Gi says that the meat must be aged between 19 and 28 days for the best flavor. The *Chianina* are huge animals that some scholars say are depicted in ancient cave dwellings. It is difficult to spot them in the countryside, and they are becoming quite rare. They are light gray in color with short horns and a broad back. After the recent mad cow epidemic in Europe it was virtually impossible to buy a T-bone steak with a bone in it, but the restrictions are slowly being lifted.

The name *bistecca* comes from a story surrounding some Englishmen who happened to be in the Piazza San Lorenzo in Florence in 1565 for a feast where the townspeople were spit-roasting beef. When the Englishmen saw the beef they began chanting "beefsteak, beefsteak" and the name resonated with the crowd, who turned the word into *bistecca*.

The fire was ready, but before Gi put the steak on she grilled pork ribs *(suino)* liberally rubbed with coarse salt for what is known as *rosticciana,* a typical pork-rib dish served separately from the *bistecca*. While the pork ribs were sizzling away, she used a rocking knife *(mezzaluna)* to make the *battuto,* or minced mixture of garlic, fine sea salt, and rosemary that is rubbed on the steak before it hits the grill. Gi meant business at that point, and whipped out her hairdryer to really get that fire hot! What she wanted to achieve was a steak that was seared on the outside but remained for the most part raw inside. As it cooked she mixed olive oil and Chianti wine together and used a little rosemary brush to baste the steak. When it was ready she cut it into thin slices and topped it with arugula. My mouth was watering as this dish was placed on a self-service buffet along with the *rosticciana,* spicy chicken *(Pollo al Mattone, p. 42)* also cooked on the grill, a huge bowl of mixed vegetables *(Tuttoinsieme, p. 44)*, and penne pasta dressed in a tomato-pesto sauce. The best of Tuscan food was now on display.

All this for us? As if answering my question, the doorbell rang and in paraded friends and neighbors. We all sat at the table in Gi's tiny kitchen where the power of food became the handshake of friendship, where glasses clinked, conversation flowed, hearty laughs filled the house, and Eduardo entertained us with his music. In a setting like this I gave silent thanks for traditions that I hope will never die, and I was happy to experience what it is like to eat like a Florentine.

Bistecca alla Fiorentina
Grilled T-Bone Steak

SERVES 4

2 cloves garlic, peeled

2 tablespoons fresh
rosemary leaves

½ teaspoon salt

1 1½-pound
T-bone steak

½ cup red wine

¼ cup extra-virgin
olive oil

1 cup arugula leaves

Before the Tuscans coined the word bistecca *(from the English "beefsteak") for a T-bone steak, it went by the name* carbonate, *literally carbon steak, since it was cooked over a charcoal flame. The meat is from Chianina (an Italian breed), and is low in fat and juicy, owing to the grasses that the cows feed on. A true bistecca is served al sangue, cooked on the outside but remains fairly raw inside. It is served with arugula or other salad greens. The dish is also called* tagliata, *meaning cut into slices.*

Fire up the grill and get it really hot.

Make a pile on a cutting board of the garlic and rosemary. Sprinkle the pile with ¼ teaspoon of the salt. Use a chef's knife, or a rocking knife called a *mezzaluna*, and finely mince the ingredients. Rub the mixture all over the steak and put it on the grill. Grill the steak until it is nicely browned on the outside but remains rare inside. Use a small knife to make an incision in the meat to determine rareness.

While the steak is cooking, combine the wine and 2 tablespoons of the olive oil. Use a brush or a rosemary sprig to baste the steak as it cooks.

In a bowl toss together the arugula, remaining olive oil, and salt.

When the steak is ready, cut it into ¼-inch-thick slices and place them on a plate. Place the arugula salad over the steak and serve.

Pesto
Basil Sauce

MAKES 2 CUPS

Pesto sauce made from fresh basil leaves and walnuts or pine nuts is traditionally used over trenette, *long strands of pasta similar to tagliatelle; but Gi likes to add it to her cherry tomato sauce for penne with* Salsa di Pomodori Ciliegini *(p. 41). It is best to use small-leaf basil if you can find it; I find the flavor is more intense. For a vivid green color that does not turn gray, dip the leaves in a pot of boiling water for about 20 seconds. Drain and dry the leaves on paper towels before making the sauce. Pesto sauce will keep in the refrigerator for a month if covered with a layer of olive oil over the top.*

⅓ cup pine nuts or walnuts

2 cups packed fresh basil leaves, stemmed

3 cloves garlic

½ cup extra-virgin olive oil

3 tablespoons grated pecorino cheese

Coarse sea salt to taste

Preheat the oven to 350°F.

Spread the nuts on a small pie plate and bake them for about 4 to 5 minutes, or until they are nicely browned. Remove the nuts from the oven and set aside to cool.

Grind the basil leaves with the garlic in a food processor until the mixture is coarse. Add the oil slowly through the feed tube, keeping the motor running until a paste begins to form. You may not need all the olive oil. The pesto should be the consistency of ketchup. Turn off the motor and add the pine nuts or walnuts and process until the nuts are in bits.

Transfer the pesto to a small bowl. Stir in the cheese and taste the pesto for saltiness. Add salt a little at a time to your liking. Remember that pecorino cheese has a salty taste, so do not oversalt the pesto.

Transfer the pesto to a jar. Pour a thin layer of olive oil over the top, cap the jar, and store in the refrigerator.

NOTE: Pesto sauce is delicious spread on toasted slices of bread for a quick *bruschetta*. Also try it on pizza and fish.

Pollo al Mattone
Chicken Cooked Under Bricks

SERVES 4

Juice of 2 lemons

2 teaspoons hot red
pepper flakes

Coarse black pepper
to taste

1½ teaspoons coarse
sea salt

4-pound roasting chicken
split in half

3 or 4 clean bricks, each
wrapped in aluminum foil

Pollo al Mattone, *chicken cooked under bricks, is said to have originated in Impruneta, the town near Florence famous all over the world for its beautifully made terra-cotta tiles. According to tradition, this dish was made for the feast of San Luca, the town's patron. The method of grilling the chicken with a weight on it allows the bird to keep contact with the grill and cook evenly. At one time, heavy terra-cotta pots were used to weigh the chicken down. Even if you do not have a fireplace grill like Gi's, you can achieve the same results on a really hot outdoor grill, heated to about 500°F.*

Prepare the grill.

In a large, shallow bowl combine the lemon juice, red pepper flakes, pepper, and salt. Coat each side of the chicken halves in the mixture, then place them directly on the grill and position the bricks on top of each half.

Grill carefully, watching and regulating the heat as is necessary to avoid flare-ups. Remove the bricks using oven mitts. Use tongs to turn the chicken once to cook on the other side. Reposition the bricks on top of the chicken. When fork-tender remove the bricks, transfer the chicken to a cutting board, and cut it into pieces. Serve hot.

To prepare a stove-top version, brown the chicken in a sauté pan in 2 tablespoons of extra-virgin olive oil. Place the bricks or other suitable weights on top of the chicken pieces. Cook over medium heat, turning the chicken pieces once during the cooking process to brown the other side.

Salsa di Pomodori Ciliegini e Pesto
Cherry Tomato–Pesto Sauce

SERVES 4 (MAKES 1½ CUPS)

As if the bistecca, pollo al mattone, *and* rosticiana *were not enough, Gi started things off with penne in a* Salsa di Pomodori Ciliegini, *or cherry tomato sauce. It was delicious and clung to the penne just right. We all gathered around the country kitchen table to enjoy it.*

Heat the olive oil in a large sauté pan and brown the garlic. Remove and discard the garlic, add the tomatoes and salt, and cook the sauce for 20 minutes uncovered. Stir in the pesto. Cover and keep the sauce warm while the penne is cooking.

Cook the penne in 4 quarts of rapidly boiling salted water until it is al dente, firm but cooked through, with not a trace of flour remaining when a piece is cut in half.

Drain the penne, reserve 2 tablespoons of the cooking water, and add the reserved water and the penne to the sauté pan with the sauce. Mix well over medium heat until heated through. Serve immediately.

¼ cup extra-virgin olive oil

2 cloves garlic, thinly sliced

1¼ pounds cherry tomatoes, cut in half

¼ teaspoon fine sea salt

4 tablespoons prepared pesto sauce (p. 41)

1 pound penne *rigate* (with lines)

Tuttoinsieme
Mixed Vegetables

2 large baking potatoes, peeled and cut into ½-inch cubes

2 medium-size zucchini, cut into chunks

2 large carrots, peeled and cut into 1-inch rounds

2 red onions, thinly sliced

1 medium fennel, white bulb only, cut into ½-inch-thick slices

¼ cup extra-virgin olive oil

Fine sea salt to taste

Coarse black pepper to taste

I love the name tuttoinsieme *(everything together). This quick mixed vegetable dish can do duty for any meat, fish, fowl, or game course.*

Put all the vegetables and the oil in a large sauté pan and cook over medium heat for 3 or 4 minutes. Cover the pan and continue cooking until the vegetables are cooked but still al dente. A knife should be able to pierce them without resistance, but the vegetables should retain their shapes. Season with salt and pepper. Serve with *Bistecca alla Fiorentina* (p. 40).

The Merchant of Prato's Biscuits

Biscotti di Prato Antonio Mattei
(Almond Cookies from the Antonio Mattei Pastry Shop)

P RATO IS A MEDIEVAL northern Tuscan city that has been important since the thirteenth century as a textile manufacturing center. But I first came to know it as the home of its most famous citizen, Francesco di Marco Datini (1335–1410), when I was preparing my masters thesis on Italian food and read the book *The Merchant of Prato* by Iris Origo. In 1870, four hundred and sixty years after Datini's death, his account ledgers, private letters, and business contracts were discovered in a hiding place beneath the staircase in his home, the Palazzo Datini. These became the subject of the book, and through them we get a fascinating look into life in the Middle Ages in Tuscany.

The Palazzo Datini on Via Rinaldesca is a museum today, and a rare example of a late–fourteenth century home. I wanted to see it, so one day I hopped on a train from Grizzana for the thirty-minute ride to the center of Prato. The palazzo, with its massive stone exterior, cannot be appreciated for its grandeur as it sits snug and wedged in among the other buildings at the edge of the street. I had to cross the street to really get a good view of the frescoes on the outside of the palazzo that recount events in Datini's life as a businessman and a patron of the city. When you walk inside you can feel his presence and sense the wealth that he had amassed in the elegantly frescoed rooms with bird and animal scenes, as well as floral motifs. I could almost hear his voice as I looked around and recalled my research of the letters he wrote to his mother in 1371 instructing her to make his favorite foods of "capons, fresh eggs, and fine fish from

Bisenzio, many good figs and peaches and nuts." And he enjoyed good wine and fine biscuits.

Making good biscuits is a tradition in Prato, and not far from Datini's palazzo is the Biscottificio Antonio Mattei on Via Ricasoli. Since 1858 it has been making one of Prato's most famous biscuits, *biscotti di Prato alla mandorla* (p. 49), similar to what Datini would have enjoyed for dunking in wine. Today, three generations of the Pandolfini family carry out the work begun by Mattei. When you walk into this pastry shop, rows of sky blue bags packaged with *biscotti alla mandorla* greet you. The clerk explained with pride that up until the mid-twentieth century, the biscotti were still being cut into their distinctive diagonal shape by hand. Now sophisticated machinery does the work so that the shop can keep up with the demand. Almonds are the beloved ingredient in just about every confection that is made here, as evidenced by beautiful confectioner's sugar–powdered cake disks called *la torta mantovana*, made with almonds and orange flavoring, and *brutti ma buoni* (ugly but good) almond-flavored cookies. Other Tuscan sweets include *il pan di ramerino* (rosemary and raisin bread), ladyfingers, chocolate-flavored brioche, and *pan di Spagna*.

I purchased two bags of cookies and headed back to the train station. It was worth the trip to satiate a sweet tooth and pay homage to Prato's favorite son, and I'd like to think that when Francesco di Marco Datini entertained his business guests he would seal any dealings with a glass of Vin Santo, into which were dipped *biscotti di Prato alla mandorla*.

Biscotti di Prato Antonio Mattei
Almond Cookies from the
Antonio Mattei Pastry Shop

MAKES 2½ DOZEN

*T*he best biscotti di Prato *come from the* Biscottificio Antonio Mattei *in Prato itself. But if you cannot get to this sweet shop anytime soon, here is the recipe to try at home. These are long-keepers and good dunkers for coffee or wine. They also make a great gift.*

⅔ cup whole almonds

2 cups unbleached all-purpose flour

1½ teaspoons baking powder

¼ teaspoon salt

¾ cup sugar

3 large eggs at room temperature

1 tablespoon vanilla extract

Preheat the oven to 350°F.

Spread the almonds on a baking sheet and toast them in the oven for about 7 minutes, or just until they begin to darken. Do not let them burn. When you begin to smell them they are done. Transfer the almonds to a bowl and allow them to cool.

Sift the flour, baking powder, and salt together in another bowl. Set aside.

In a separate bowl whisk together the sugar, eggs, and vanilla. Stir this into the flour mixture and use your hands to form a dough. Work in the almonds. The dough will be stiff.

Flour your hands and transfer the dough to a sheet of waxed paper. Shape the dough into a 10 × 5½-inch-long loaf. Wrap the dough in the waxed paper and refrigerate it for several hours or even overnight.

Use a sharp knife to cut the dough in half lengthwise, reshape each half into a loaf, and place the loaves 2 inches apart on a parchment-lined baking sheet.

Bake the loaves for about 18 minutes, or until they are firm to the touch and browned. Remove the baking sheet from the oven and allow the loaves to cool for 15 minutes.

Use a sharp knife to cut diagonal ½-inch-thick slices from each loaf. Place the slices back on the baking sheet and return them to the oven to toast for about 8 minutes, or until they are nicely browned.

Remove the baking sheet from the oven and transfer the biscotti to a cooling rack. As they cool they will crisp even more. The texture of this cookie should be dry and crumbly.

VARIATION: To make miniature biscotti, divide the dough into quarters and form into loaves. Bake as directed, but reduce the baking time by about 4 minutes.

San Sepolcro's Secrets

Pancetta di Maiale in Porchetta Da Ventura
(Roast Pork Da Ventura Style)

Patate con Olio e Ramerino
(Potatoes with Olive Oil and Rosemary)

Salsicce con l'uve
(Sweet Pork Sausages with Grapes)

BOTTICELLI BLUE SKIES and porcelain white clouds set the day's tone for visiting San Sepolcro, an industrial town in eastern Tuscany. This definitely is not a tourist destination, but for me there were two reasons to visit: the food at Da Ventura (which I will get to in a minute) and a well-kept secret, a fresco of the Resurrection, the magnificent work of native-born artist, Piero della Francesca (1410–1492), which is housed in the Museo Civico. I first saw it years ago, and was so stunned by its compelling power and grace that I knew I had to see it again. It depicts a stoic-looking, triumphant Christ dressed in light, rose-colored robes standing with his foot on the tomb, and the flag of victory in his hand, while Romans soldiers dressed in Renaissance garb sleep at his feet. Piero, in a self-portrait, is there, too, a hatless person sleeping to the left of the risen Christ. Both times I have seen this magnificent fresco, it has been all mine; there are no crowds to mar the view or the contemplation. It is my secret pleasure.

Da Ventura is a one-fork restaurant, meaning it rates very high among restaurant critics who use the three-fork system to evaluate the best restaurants in Italy. To get even one fork is a big deal, so wanting to film there was a no-brainer. I called the restaurant from my cell phone and hoped that someone would answer. In Italy, Monday is an iffy day for a lot of restaurants that take the day off as a reprieve for working on weekends. On the third ring a voice answered and I asked for Giuliano Tofanelli, the owner of Da Ventura, whom I met several years ago when I stopped for lunch. No, he was not in, but his son

Marco was. So I spoke with him and told him that the food was so memorable there that I wanted to bring the film crew to do a show about it. At first Marco seemed stunned, but when I told him it would be great publicity for him, he agreed. When we arrived with all our equipment, Marco Tofanelli greeted us cordially, not sure what to expect from a television crew. He is of slight build and seems shy, the exact opposite of his boisterous father. I hoped that he would not freeze in front of the camera. I asked if he would recreate the *pancetta di maiale in porchetta* that I had on my last visit. This is the most delicious pork roast, with a crackling skin so crispy that it needs to be cut with a scissors after it is cooked. "*No problema,*" Marco assured me, since this is a staple on the menu, and he started to get the ingredients ready.

Da Ventura was just as I remembered it—a cozy place where mostly locals come, and they like it that way. On the walls are black-and-white caricatures done by famed local artist Alberto Fremura, who has captured the personalities of world figures from Charles de Gaulle to George Bush to Frank Sinatra.

In the center of the restaurant was a huge antipasto table resplendent with platters of marinated artichoke hearts, zucchini, and eggplant. There were thin slices of the local *salame,* goat and pecorino cheeses, glistening cantaloupe, gigantic green olives, colorful mixed pepper chunks, and *lonzina di maiale*, which is cured pork tenderloin cut in paper-thin slices. Hunger began to set in, but I knew there was work to do first.

Having worked in many restaurant kitchens in Italy, I am always astounded that so much food can be turned out in such a small work space. For that reason, making pasta typically takes place outside the kitchen area.

Marina, the *sfoglina* (a name given to women whose sole job it is to turn out homemade pasta), was making ravioli. She has been doing this since she was eight, as evidenced by the speed with which she rolled a round of dough out with a broom handle–size rolling pin into a thin bed sheet and filled it with a mixture of pureed spinach, fresh ricotta cheese, grated Parmigiano-Reggiano cheese, cinnamon, nutmeg, salt, and white pepper. She cuts ravioli shapes the size of postage stamps while proudly telling me that she used ten eggs for a kilo of flour (about 2¼ pounds) to make the dough. Like Marina, the *sfoglina* is usually middle-aged, and I know with their passing the tradition of making pasta *casalinga* (homemade) will also fade.

Marco was ready for his scene, so I squeezed into the tiny kitchen area with the camera crew. It was only a few hours until lunch time, when the kitchen had to have everything ready for hungry patrons, so we needed to work efficiently and fast. I could tell that Marco was a little nervous about the camera, but his fears were allayed as he began to concentrate on the dish and rubbed the pork with aromatic spices of fennel flower *(fiori di finocchio),* salt, pepper, and garlic. In about two hours I would be reliving one of the best gastronomic secrets of this Tuscan kitchen.

When we finished shooting the scene, Marco invited us to have lunch. We began with selections from the antipasto table, then sampled Marina's

Marco Tofanelli explains the process for making pancetta di maiale in porchetta, *that succulent pork roast with the crackling bronze skin!*

light-as-a-feather ravioli. The crescendo of anticipation grew for the pork brought to our table, filled with the aroma of fennel and garlic. Our waiter cut into the skin with a scissors and it crackled like a sheet of rumpled waxed paper. One taste confirmed once again why Da Ventura is a one-fork restaurant. As an added show of hospitality Marco rolled out *stinco di vitello,* a whole veal shank that begged us to lick our fingers after devouring the tender and juicy meat.

For me this was the perfect day, with Botticelli blue skies, white porcelain clouds, a taste of *pancetta di maiale in porchetta,* and a visit to the Museo Civico, the best kept secret in San Sepolcro.

Pancetta di Maiale in Porchetta Da Ventura
Roast Pork Da Ventura Style

SERVES 10 TO 12

6½ pound boneless center-cut loin pork roast, or sirloin roast, butterflied

2 knobs of garlic, separated into cloves and left unpeeled (about 12 to 15 cloves)

2 to 3 tablespoons fine sea salt

Coarse ground black pepper to taste

1 tablespoon ground fennel seeds or fennel pollen (see note on page 57)

Extra pork fat

4 fennel tops with stems

*T*his incredible pork roast, known as pancetta di maiale in porchetta, *was worth the trip to San Sepolcro, where chef Marco Tofanelli made it for me just as I had remembered his father preparing it years ago at Da Ventura. Pancetta refers to pork from the belly of the pig. The flavor is sweeter than our pork and the meat must marinate for two days to meld the seasonings. To achieve the crispy exterior, ask your butcher to give you extra pork fat for placing on top of the meat, as American pork is much leaner than the Italian equivalent. This is a great holiday main entree, and the next best thing to being at Da Ventura.*

When you get the roast home from the butcher, open it like a book. Flatten the garlic cloves slightly with the back of a knife and sprinkle them randomly over the meat. It may seem like a lot of garlic, but you will be surprised at how mild the flavor will be. Sprinkle the salt, and a grinding of black pepper evenly over the meat, then sprinkle on the ground fennel seeds or fennel pollen. Now roll the meat up tightly like a jelly roll. Spread the extra pork fat on top of the roast. Put the whole fennel leaves on top of the pork fat, and anchor everything in place by tying it in several places with kitchen string.

Put the roast in a pan, cover it with aluminum foil, and put it in the refrigerator to marinate for two days. Marco says that this is critical to developing the flavors.

When you are ready to cook, preheat the oven to 325°F. Put the roast in a roasting pan and cook it on the middle oven rack for 1½ hours, then raise the temperature to 425°F and cook 1 hour longer. The roast should be almost bronze-looking.

Cut the strings and discard them along with the fennel tops.

Let the roast stand for 5 or 10 minutes covered. It will slice better if you are patient. Cut the roast into serving slices and accompany with potatoes with olive oil and rosemary (p. 58).

NOTE: Marco used *fiore di finocchio*, or fennel flower, to flavor the pork. I bought some in a small grocery store in San Sepolcro. You can substitute ground fennel seeds by placing whole fennel seeds in a small grinder. Or you can buy something called fennel pollen in speciality stores or through catalogs such as Penzey's.

Patate con Olio e Ramerino
Potatoes with Olive Oil and Rosemary

SERVES 4 TO 6

2 pounds Russet potatoes, peeled and cut into 1-inch chunks

⅓ cup extra-virgin olive oil

2 tablespoons minced rosemary leaves

1½ teaspoons fine sea salt

Coarse black pepper to taste

*W*hat goes with *pancetta di maiale in porchetta (p. 56)? Why, pan-roasted potatoes with rosemary! At Da Ventura the potatoes are parboiled before being tossed into a large skillet and cooked quickly on the stove top. Use a starchy type of potato, such as Russet.*

Put the potato chunks in a pot and cover them with cold water. Add 1 teaspoon of the salt and bring them to a boil. Cook the potatoes just until a knife easily pierces them, about 3 to 4 minutes. Drain the potatoes in a colander and set aside.

Heat the olive oil in a large skillet, or lacking that, use two smaller pans or cook the potatoes in batches. It is important that the potatoes have contact with the surface of the pan or they will not brown evenly.

Add the potatoes with the rosemary and cook them, turning occasionally so they brown evenly. Toss the potatoes gently with the remaining salt and pepper and serve as a side dish with *Pancetta di Maiale in Porchetta Da Ventura* (p. 56)

NOTE: In Tuscany, rosemary is called *ramerino,* and is a favorite herb used with meat and potato dishes. Twist several branches of rosemary together to create a Tuscan "basting brush" to use while grilling meats as they cook, which also imparts the rosemary flavor.

Salsicce con l'uve
Sweet Pork Sausages with Grapes

SERVES 4

*T*wo *ingredients, sweet sausage and grapes, are all you need to prepare this impressive-looking company dish. Use good sweet or hot sausage; both are good with sugary grapes.*

Poke the sausages with a fork and put them in a sauté pan with ½ cup of water. Cook the sausages uncovered over medium heat until they turn gray. Drain off the water. Allow the sausages to brown in their own fat, turning them once or twice. If they are very lean, add a tablespoon of olive oil to the pan. Five minutes before the sausage is cooked, add the grapes to the pan and cook for 2 or 3 minutes longer. Transfer to a serving dish.

Serve very hot.

1 pound homemade or store-bought Italian sausage

2 cups mixed seedless red and green grapes, each cut in half

How to Read a Tuscan Menu

No visitor to Tuscany, or any other region of Italy, wants to feel intimidated by a menu. If you don't speak the language, much less read it, how is a discriminating traveler to know what to order?

It is true that in most restaurants the menu will be given in English as well as in Italian, but this is not always the case, especially when traveling around to small towns and villages. It is usually my job to decipher the menu for the *Ciao Italia* crew so they know what to expect from their dining experience.

In large cities most restaurants post their menus, with prices, outside. If a large-city restaurant does not post its menu, avoid it. In smaller towns where there is little tourism there often is no posting since the "menu" is whatever is the whim of the chef that day. These out-of-the-way eateries can be some of the best places to enjoy authentic food.

Once you have decided on a restaurant, study the menu and choose things that are typical of the region: In the case of Tuscany order such classics as *Bistecca alla Fiorentina* (p. 40) for a main entree instead of a pizza or spaghetti with tomato sauce, two dishes belonging to the region of Campania in the south. Dishes not typical of the region may be on the menu, but avoid them if you want to eat as the locals do. Please do not ask the wait staff if there are American dishes such as roast beef and hamburgers. Many people do just that, and it is an insult to your host country.

One of the first things you will see on a Tuscan menu are the words *pane e coperto* (bread and cover) meaning that there is a charge to sit down at the table as well as a charge for the bread brought to your table. Your table belongs to you for as long as you wish to sit there, even after you have lingered over espresso at the end of the meal and the line for the next diners is out the door. No one will shoo you out.

When Tuscans eat in restaurants they do so in a succession of courses. Unlike the American dinner plate sporting meat, vegetables, and perhaps a starch all crowded together, Tuscans will start out with an antipasto of cured meats such as prosciutto, or their beloved local *finocchiona,* dried sausage studded with fennel seeds, or maybe *fettunta,* grilled bread rubbed with garlic and drizzled with extra-virgin olive oil. The first course, called a *primo piatto,* is next and can be soup like *ribollita* (p. 210), or pasta such as *pappardelle* (p. 22), tagliatelle (p. 153), or *pinci* (p. 119). The second course *(secondo piatto)* brings a choice of meats like *cinghiale* (p. 20), or duck, fish such as *triglia* (p. 113) and poultry, such as *Pollo al Mattone* (p. 42) with *contorni,* or vegetable side dishes, that might include green vegetables of the season, such as Swiss chard or fried zucchini flowers. Green salad is a separate course, usually served after the meat course and dressed with extra-virgin olive oil, good wine vinegar, and salt. Don't expect croutons, grated cheese, or bottled dressings. During the course of the meal, wine and bottled water, either still or carbonated, is served.

In finer restaurants a cheese course may be offered, and in Tuscany the choices might include locally produced pecorino cheeses, young or aged like *marzolino* or *caciotta.*

Most often, dessert is an assortment of fresh whole fruits in season, such as pears, figs, melon, strawberries, apples, oranges, and grapes brought to your table in a bowl of water. Use a knife to cut away the skin of oranges and cut apples into segments. Use a fork, not your hands, to eat these fruits. For sturdier desserts *(dolci)* there may be biscotti, gelato, fruit tarts, or *zuccotto* (p. 190), a classic rich Tuscan trifle.

When your bill *(conto)* arrives, study it carefully. In Italy the service *(servizio)* and taxes are already included in your meal price, so there is no need to leave a tip unless you feel that the waitstaff and the kitchen have gone out of their way to please you. You can leave an additional tip as a sign of your gratitude if you wish.

Once you know the basics of the Tuscan menu, you're bound to have a memorable meal.

Lucca's Legacy

Buccellato di Lucca (Raisin-Anise Bread)

Buccellato alle Fragole e Mascarpone
(Layered Raisin-Anise Bread with
Strawberries and Mascarpone)

ANCIENT ROME left its mark on Lucca, in northern Tuscany, when the city was claimed as a Roman colony in 180 B.C. I am reminded of this every time I step inside this quaint, walled city and walk to one of its finest landmarks, the Anfiteatro Romano, or old Roman amphitheater, the shape of which still outlines Piazza del Mercato, a visible reminder of Lucca's legacy.

Lucca has other distinctive landmarks as well. For example, not many cities can boast a tower with oak trees growing on its top, but such is the case in Lucca. The tower is also a reminder of the Giungi family, one of the most powerful to rule Lucca in the fifteenth century. The tree-topped tower served as a watch post, guarding against enemies, like the Medici family of Florence, who were never able to conquer and claim the city. And then there is the fabulous church of San Michele in Foro, whose name indicates that it stands on the site of the old Roman forum. Its Romanesque style with richly decorated columns reminds me of icing on an elaborately decorated wedding cake. San Martino, Lucca's cathedral, rivals that of San Michele in Foro with its beautiful carved, marble facade depicting Saint Martin on horseback, dressed as a Roman soldier and dividing his cloak with a sword to give it to a beggar. Inside, the cathedral houses the tomb of Ilaria del Carretto, the young wife of Paolo Giungi, and is one of the most endearing tombs I have ever seen. Her carved likeness is that of a child bride, dressed in elegant robes, her sweet face frozen in perpetual sleep.

If you like opera, you might want to visit the home of Giacomo Puccini, who was born here in 1858. Opera lovers flock to his house, now a museum, where he was composing the music to *Turandot* before his death.

For food, make it a point to stroll along Via Fillungo, Lucca's main shopping street. Here you will find old grocery stores and pastry shops selling the specialties of the area, including Lucca's superior extra-virgin olive oils, chestnut flour, and chestnut cakes, *torta co' becchi*, pastry dough that is filled with Swiss chard, and its signature ring-shaped sweet bread, *buccellato* (p. 67), that can be as large as a wagon wheel. It is said that the Lucchesi buy this bread for special occasions, including to give to children on their confirmation. It is very rarely made at home, and you must get to the pastry shop early in order to reserve one, or find yourself bitterly disappointed when the last one leaves the store. Over time the ingredients for this bread have evolved; modern versions are packed with raisins and diced candied fruits, while traditional ones are flavored with aniseeds, a practice going back to the Middle Ages, when it was thought that these tiny licorice-flavored seeds had spiritual power over evil spells. Perhaps that is why biting into a slice of *bucellatto* can be, in a word, divine.

Buccellato di Lucca
Raisin-Anise Bread

MAKES ONE LARGE RING

Buccellato Taddeucci in Lucca sells this sweet bread that is said to have been a favorite of the ancient Roman army, and in fact are sometimes made as large as a Roman cart's wheel. Buccellato is the standard confirmation gift to children from their grandparents.

Dissolve the yeast in the water in a large bowl. Stir in the milk, 2 eggs, sugar, and butter. Stir in 2 cups of the flour, raisins, aniseeds, and salt. Add the remaining flour a little at a time until a soft ball of dough is created. Place the dough in a lightly greased bowl, cover tightly with plastic wrap, and allow it to rise for 1 hour.

Preheat the oven to 375°F.

Transfer the dough to a floured surface and punch it down with your fists. Knead the dough for a few minutes, then roll it out into a 32-inch rope and bring the ends together to form a ring shape. Place the ring on a lightly buttered cookie sheet. Cover with a clean towel and allow it to rise until almost doubled.

Brush the dough with the remaining egg and bake until golden brown, about 35 to 40 minutes. Remove the *buccellato* to a cooling rack to cool completely.

NOTE: To keep the center of the ring open during baking, place a well-buttered custard-type dish in the center of the ring. After the bread is baked and cooled carefully remove the dish.

1 package active dried yeast

½ cup warm water (110°F)

1 cup warm milk (110°F)

3 large eggs at room temperature

½ cup sugar

4 tablespoons unsalted butter at room temperature

6 to 6¼ cups unbleached all-purpose flour

1 cup raisins

1 tablespoon aniseeds, crushed

1 teaspoon fine salt

Buccellato alle Fragole e Mascarpone
Layered Raisin-Anise Bread with Strawberries and Mascarpone

SERVES 8

1 pound ripe strawberries, stemmed and cut into slices

⅓ cup sugar

Juice of 1 large lemon

5 cups dry red wine

24 slices of *buccellato*, or enough to fill a 9 × 13-inch glass pan to make three layers

1 cup whipping cream

¼ cup mascarpone or cream cheese at room temperature

2 tablespoons confectioner's sugar

Mint leaves for garnish

Let's just say that you have too much of a good buccellato *on hand. What to do? Make this sensational layered dessert with slices of the bread (either fresh or stale) soaked in a strawberry-wine sauce.*

Mash the berries in a large bowl with a fork. Stir in the sugar and lemon juice. Pour in the wine and mix well. Cover the bowl and refrigerate the mixture for 3 hours.

Line the pan with 8 slices of *buccellato,* trimming them if necessary to fit the pan. Cover the slices with some of the wine sauce. Make two more alternating layers of bread and sauce, ending with the sauce mixture on top. Cover the pan and refrigerate for several hours to allow the bread to absorb all the liquid.

Whip the cream with the mascarpone or cream cheese and sugar until stiff.

When ready to serve, cut the *buccellato* into serving-size pieces, like lasagne. Place them on individual dessert dishes and top with some of the whipped cream. Add a mint leaf for garnish and serve.

Dinner in a Palazzino

Fagioli al Fiasco (Beans Cooked in a Flask)

Fagioli all'Uccelletto
(Bird-Style Stewed Beans)

Insalata con Quattro Formaggi
(Salad with Four Cheeses)

Polpettine alla Iris (Iris's Tuscan Meatballs)

Polpette di Ricotta alla Lulu San Angelo
(Lulu San Angelo's Ricotta Cheese Meatballs)

*Straccetti e Cannellini con la Salsa di
Olio di Oliva*
(Iris's Pasta Fantasia with Fresh Cannellini
Beans and Olive Sauce)

Zuppa Lombarda
(Soup for the Lombards)

M Y GOOD FRIENDS Iris and Gioni Lodovici know how and where to live . . . right in the center of Florence in Palazzo Corona. Gioni is a well-known author on the subject of wine, and Iris is a fabulous cook. Together they make a striking team, and they always teach me something new. Why not capture them on film in their respective elements and give our television audience a behind-the-scenes look at life in their small palazzo (*palazzino*), I thought.

Iris was born in Florence, and in her eyes she is living a Renaissance life amidst the treasures and wonders of the city, knowing that she will never see it all. For her Florence *is* the center of the universe. In awe of its art, architecture, history, and music, she has no desire to be anywhere else but in her *palazzino*.

Gioni, also a Florentine, was born just a few meters from the famous *duomo,* Florence's magnificent cathedral. His enthusiasm for making wine and olive oil on his country estate called Poggio D'Oglio, not far from Florence, pervades everything he does.

Inside their beautifully appointed *palazzino,* furnished with gorgeous antiques, the place to look is up, at the exquisitely painted angelic scenes on the ceiling of a small chapel, my favorite room. On the day I arrived, the excitement was all due to tiny birds that had hatched between the window and the outside wall of the chapel! A good-luck sign, according to Iris.

In the kitchen Iris is a whiz. She views cooking as a passion, while Gioni takes a scholarly approach, researching the importance of wine. And he has set rules about the foods of Italy as well. Don't even think of putting grated cheese on pasta dishes, he warns me. This is forbidden in the Lodovici kitchen, since he believes cheeses should be enjoyed on their own where the taste is not lost among competing flavors.

Everything was ready for the camera to roll. Knowing how animated Iris always seemed whenever I visited, I knew there would be no trouble getting her to talk about the recipes that we were about to make. But suddenly she announced that she was going to take a short nap! So I settled myself into a cozy armchair and waited.

The food in question that day was *cannellini* beans, a Florentine staple that no serious Tuscan cook would overlook. Beans are to Tuscany what rice is to northern Italy and pasta is to southern Italy.

Fresh as a daisy from her nap, Iris was ready to make *straccetti* (p. 80), small, irregular pieces of fresh, flat pasta that she combines with fresh *cannellini* beans and a sauce made with parsley and olives. Flour, eggs, and a pinch of salt are all that go into making the bright yellow dough. Iris tells me this color is due to the natural feed given to the hens. The dish was elegant in its simplicity, and healthy, too.

Next came *cannellini* beans *all'uccelletto* (p. 75), in the style of small birds, so called because they are traditionally served alongside small cooked birds and use the same ingredients to make *Fagioli al Fiasco* except for the tomatoes. The beans were so creamy that they almost dissolved on the tongue. Who would think that something as common as white beans could elicit such raves!

The hour was growing late as we wrapped up the film segment, and Iris and Gioni insisted that we all stay for dinner to sample the bean dishes. We were shooed like a flock of birds out of the kitchen and into the dining room where the table was set with fine linen and Iris's best china. Sitting down I noticed a lineup at each place setting of several wineglasses and forks. This dinner was not going to be just about beans!

Gioni arrived with a huge platter of marinated tiny octopus and diced potatoes, all sprinkled with fish eggs. Iris entered behind him with a warm arugula salad (the tender, young leaves were from Gioni's garden) served with a mixture of melted cheeses, black olives, olive oil, and balsamic vinegar. The *stracetti* with those creamy beans were next . . . and there was more. Tiny, fried Tuscan meatballs served in a *besciamella* sauce with mushrooms and parsley were unusual and very tasty.

Dessert was *baba au rhum* (sponge cake soaked in rum) sitting in an ethereal, perfect puddle of pastry cream. I scraped every bit off my plate. Magnificent! Not to be outdone, Gioni's passionate knowledge of wine resulted in our being served several elegant varieties from his own cellar. We sampled Sangiovese and cabernet from the 1997 to the 2001 vintages. As a surprise he saved the best for last, and played a game where we had to guess the vintage year of the Vin Santo he was about

Iris puts the final touches on stracetti.

to uncork. From the looks of the bottle, and knowing how serious he was about wine, I guessed that it was about sixty years old. It was in fact a 1950 vintage, with an interesting story. It seems the wine was preserved in a barrel during World War II, then bottled in 1950. He opened it with great ceremony as if he were pouring for royalty, which of course we felt like in our surroundings.

Over that dessert wine the conversation lingered long into the evening, and I thought how wonderful it was to be part of such gracious hospitality. Finally, it was time to leave what had been a dreamy day, and I have to agree with Iris: If I lived in Florence, my *palazzino* would be my world, too.

Fagioli al Fiasco
Beans Cooked in a Flask

1½ pounds fresh
cannellini beans

½ cup extra-virgin
olive oil

6 whole sage leaves

2 cloves garlic, peeled

1 tablespoon sea salt

1 teaspoon coarse
black pepper

3 cups water

*F*resh and dried beans are a signature staple in the Tuscan diet. *They are nutritious and cost very little, and they are used ingeniously in cooking.* Cannellini *and* toscanelli *are two white beans that Tuscans favor. An intriguing way of preparing them fresh is* fagioli al fiasco, *or beans cooked in an old wine bottle with olive oil, sage, black pepper, and water. The bottle is placed over hot embers and the flask sealed with a piece of cloth. There they cook for several hours and are then served seasoned with salt. A less dramatic version is to cook them in a bean pot or other heavy-duty oven pot. Serve as a side dish to accompany meats and poultry.*

Preheat the oven to 275°F.

Put everything in the pot. Cover and bake slowly about 3 hours, or until the liquid has evaporated. Serve hot.

Fagioli all'Uccelletto
Bird-Style Stewed Beans

All'uccelletto, *or "bird-style," refers to fresh* cannellini *beans cooked with tomato paste and sage and served as the accompaniment to small game birds. Since most of us do not have the luxury of having fresh* cannellini *beans on hand, dried ones can be substituted. The dish, simple as it is, is delicately creamy and light.*

Cover the beans with cold water and allow them to soak overnight. Drain the beans, place them in a pot, cover them with fresh water, and cook them until the skins easily slip off when pressed between your fingers. Drain the beans, reserving ¼ cup of the cooking liquid, and set aside.

Heat the olive oil in a sauté pan, add the sage and cook over very low heat for 5 minutes. Stir in the beans and tomato paste dissolved in the reserved cooking liquid. Heat through. Season with salt and pepper and serve the beans with a drizzle of olive oil over the top.

2 cups dried *cannellini* or Great Northern beans

½ cup extra-virgin olive oil

5 to 6 fresh sage leaves, minced

6 tablespoons tomato paste

Salt and pepper to taste

Insalata con Quattro Formaggi
Salad with Four Cheeses

SERVES 4 TO 6

3 tablespoons extra-virgin olive oil

¼ pound *taleggio* (or fontina) cheese, cut into thin slices

¼ pound aged pecorino cheese, grated

¼ pound Swiss cheese, grated

¼ pound young pecorino (or provolone), cut into thin strips

Coarse black pepper to taste

3 cups mixed greens, washed, dried, and cut into thin strips

1½ tablespoons balsamic vinegar

Fine sea salt to taste

This intriguing salad, made with four cheeses melted over greens picked from Gioni's country garden, was so fabulous that I had to have a second helping. It is a perfect example of Iris's ingenuity in the kitchen. She uses two types of pecorino cheese, one aged and one young, along with taleggio, *a square, creamy cheese from Lombardy that is high in fat. If you cannot find* taleggio *use fontina, and for the young pecorino, substitute provolone.*

Preheat the oven to 350°F.

Brush a baking dish with one teaspoon of the olive oil. Layer the cheeses in the dish in the order given. Drizzle one teaspoon of the olive oil over the top of the cheeses and give it a grinding of black pepper.

Cover the dish with a sheet of aluminum foil and place in the oven to melt the cheese; this should take no more than 5 minutes.

Meanwhile, toss the greens in a salad bowl with the remaining olive oil and balsamic vinegar. Add a pinch of salt if you wish, but remember there is salt in the cheeses.

Transfer the greens to a platter. Scoop the cheese carefully out of the baking dish and place on top of the salad. Serve at once.

VARIATION: Add thin slices of black olives between the layers of cheese before putting the dish in the oven.

Polpettine alla Iris
Iris's Tuscan Meatballs

MAKES 8 TO 10 AS A SECOND COURSE
OR 24 AS PART OF AN ANTIPASTO

When Iris made her delicate olive-size polpettine (little meat-balls) and served them as an antipasto I felt honored, because in an Italian home you would not be served them unless you were considered family. Meatballs are the ultimate comfort food, and a part of true casalinga (home) cooking. They originated as a holdover from the days when there was little refrigeration, making it necessary to use up leftover meat trimmings, or boiled meats that had been used to make broth. So polpette (meatballs) were born. While their ingredients may vary, one thing is certain: You will never be served a dish of spaghetti with meatballs in Italy, since they are traditionally a second course served apart from the pasta course. The following is my adaptation of Iris's recipe. To make the job simple, everything can be prepared using a food processor; as Iris cautions, the secret to the tender texture is to grind everything very fine.

Grind the roast beef, mortadella, and parsley in a food processor until it is very fine. Transfer the mixture to a large bowl.

Drain the water from the porcini and pat them dry. Chop them coarsely, then melt the butter in a small sauté pan and cook them for 2 or 3 minutes before adding the meat. Stir in the eggs, cheese, nutmeg, salt, pepper, and the *besciamella* sauce. Mix all the ingredients until well combined.

Use about ¼ cup of the meat mixture to form each meatball. Place them on a baking sheet. Make meatballs smaller if desired.

Place some flour on a plate.

Lightly roll each meatball in the flour; shake off the excess and place on a platter. Cover and refrigerate them for at least 1 hour.

Heat 3 cups of the oil in a deep fryer or heavy-duty pot, and when the oil registers 375°F it is ready for frying.

¾ pound cooked roast beef

¼ pound (4 slices) mortadella with black peppercorns or pistachio nuts

¼ cup parsley leaves

¼ cup dried porcini mushrooms soaked in ½ cup warm water

1 tablespoon unsalted butter

2 large eggs, lightly beaten

¼ cup grated Parmigiano-Reggiano cheese

¼ teaspoon ground nutmeg

½ teaspoon salt

Coarse black pepper to taste

½ cup prepared *besciamella* sauce (p. 138)

Flour for coating meatballs

Extra-virgin olive oil for frying

Fry the meatballs a few at a time in the oil until they are golden brown. Remove with a slotted spoon to a paper towel–lined tray to drain.

Serve the meatballs warm on a bed of arugula leaves.

NOTE: Iris uses olive oil to fry the meatballs but sunflower oil works well, too, and gives a slightly lighter taste. Iris says the meatballs will cook faster if you use a small skillet.

Polpette di Ricotta alla Lulu San Angelo

Lulu San Angelo's Ricotta Cheese Meatballs

SERVES 8 (MAKES 12)

Making good, moist meatballs eludes many cooks. So many versions exist, including the polpettine *(p. 77), that Iris Lodovici served us in her Tuscan kitchen. Making good meatballs became a theme of one of the shows in the Tuscan series, and we invited home cooks to send us their favorite recipes. One that intrigued me was Lulu San Angelo's meatballs made with ricotta cheese. I invited her to come to the studio and make them for our television audience. Lulu is an Italian American with a large family that loves her meatballs made very moist by the addition of ricotta cheese.*

1 cup seasoned Italian bread crumbs

¾ cup whole, ½-milk, or skim-milk ricotta cheese

2 pounds ground chuck

2 large eggs, slightly beaten

½ cup minced parsley

3 cloves minced garlic

⅓ cup grated Parmigiano-Reggiano cheese

1 teaspoon fine sea salt

Coarse black pepper to taste

Preheat the oven to 350°F.

In a large bowl, mix all the ingredients gently with wet hands. Keep hands wet as you form the meatballs to prevent them from sticking to your hands. Scoop up about ⅔ cup of the meat to make each one.

Place the meatballs on a rimmed baking sheet lightly coated with olive oil and bake them for 20 to 30 minutes, or until cooked through. Serve hot.

Straccetti e Cannellini con la Salsa di Olio di Oliva

Iris's Pasta Fantasia with Fresh *Cannellini* Beans and Olive Sauce

SERVES 4 TO 6

1 recipe *pappardelle* noodles (p. 22)

½ cup dried *cannellini* or Great Northern beans, soaked overnight in water

SAUCE

20 oil-cured black olives, pitted

4 large basil leaves

½ cup flat-leaf parsley

1 tablespoon pine nuts

1 large clove garlic

½ teaspoon fine sea salt

Coarse black pepper to taste

¼ cup extra-virgin olive oil

This dish is a fantasia, *meaning that it is not a traditional Tuscan dish, but one that Iris created using elements of Tuscan cooking, in this case,* cannellini *beans. Iris makes pasta she calls* straccetti *with flour and eggs. The name, which means "tatters" or "rags," comes from cutting the dough into irregular pieces. Use the recipe on p. 22 for* pappardelle *to make the dough. Or buy packaged* pappardelle *noodles and break them up into rough 1-inch pieces before boiling.*

After rolling and cutting the dough into wide strips, use a knife and cut the strips crosswise into 1-inch pieces or into triangular pieces. Place the pieces on lightly floured towels and allow them to dry for about 1 hour before cooking. If you want to make and store the *straccetti* for future use, allow the pieces to dry until they are brittle, then store them in a sealed glass container and use within a month.

Drain the water from the beans and put them in a small pot. Cover the beans with 2 cups of fresh water and add 1 teaspoon of sea salt. Cook until the skins easily slip off the beans. Drain, set aside, and keep warm.

Mince the olives, basil leaves, parsley leaves, pine nuts, and garlic together on a cutting board. Transfer the mixture to a large pasta bowl and set aside.

Bring a large pot of water to a boil, stir in 1 tablespoon of sea salt. Add the *straccetti* and cook just until al dente. Drain off the water, reserving 2 tablespoons, and transfer the *straccetti* and the reserved water to the bowl with the olive mixture. Stir in the beans, salt, pepper, and olive oil. Serve at once.

Zuppa Lombarda
Soup for the Lombards

SERVES 6 TO 8

According to Iris, this soup was created for twelfth-century Lombard mercenary soldiers descending from Milan into Florence. They took up residence in osterie (inns) offering food and lodging. The innkeepers, surprised by the number of unexpected guests, fed them by making a soup from dried beans, stale bread, and herbs. Ever frugal, they even used the water that the beans cooked in as the broth. I have experimented with allowing the beans to soak overnight and then briefly boiling them before finishing the soup in the oven. Done this way, the beans are creamy and smooth and the broth a surprising rich color.

Soak the beans overnight; drain them, put them in a pot, cover with 6 cups of cold water, and cook them for 20 minutes. Set them aside but do not drain.

Preheat the oven to 350°F.

Heat the olive oil in a Dutch oven–type pot or other oven-proof pot. Stir in the garlic and sage and cook until the garlic softens. Stir in the tomatoes and cook for a couple of minutes. Add the beans with their cooking water and additional water to cover the beans if necessary.

Cover the pot and bake the soup until the beans are tender, about 1 hour. Place a slice of bread in each individual soup bowl and ladle the soup over the bread. Add salt and pepper to taste. Pass olive oil to drizzle on top.

1 cup dried *cannellini*, white kidney, or Great Northern beans

½ cup extra-virgin olive oil

3 cloves garlic, minced

6 to 8 fresh sage leaves, torn into pieces

2 plum tomatoes, diced

Reserved bean cooking water

6 to 8 slices toasted bread

1½ teaspoons fine sea salt

Coarse black pepper to taste

Palazzo Davanzati

Fichi Ripieni Davanzati
(Stuffed Figs Davanzati Style)

WHEN THE WORK of filming *Ciao Italia* on location is done each day, I like to take time and explore out-of-the-way places like Palazzo Davanzati in Florence. I was walking along Via Porta Rossa when I spotted it. This typical fourteenth-century house, lived in by a succession of wealthy Florentines until the nineteenth century, gives a fascinating picture of what life was like for the powerful and privileged.

Built around 1350 for the Davizzi family with stones from the nearby hills surrounding Florence, the house is a rare example of the Florentine style of the period. The entrance, or *loggia,* runs the complete length of the façade. It was used for private functions like weddings and funerals and was also the place where business deals were contracted. The *loggia* led to the courtyard, which for this palazzo was created for defensive purposes. When the door was closed the family remained safe from any outside dangers that might occur on the street, because many wealthy families also had many enemies, all vying for power.

The first floor was called the *piano nobile*, and was a gathering place for special family events. The second floor became the living quarters, but what truly intrigued me was to learn that the kitchen occupied the top floor! This made perfect sense if you think about the possibility of fire, which was common in those days since there was always an open fire going in the kitchen (at night it was covered with charcoal). Locating the kitchen at the top allowed for smoke and cooking smells to dissipate outside instead of permeating the other rooms in the house, and if a fire did occur it would be confined to the upper story and would not damage the lower ones.

Not surprisingly, the women of the house spent a lot of time in the kitchen, preparing meals, washing clothes, weaving, and ironing. It was very rare for women to leave the house except to attend mass or a festival, and they never went to market—only the men did that! Provisions for the household included cooking oils and meat bought in large quantities, which was then salted and peppered to preserve it and kept in storage areas. Oftentimes it spoiled, which led to the use of spices and sauces.

From old manuscripts in the Davanzati library a picture begins to emerge of the kinds of foods that were prepared. Some of them seem surprisingly modern, like the recipe for *fichi ripieni* (p. 87), stuffed figs. There were also stranger-sounding dishes, like a shrimp tart made with herbs, and a paste made from ground almonds, spices, and raisins.

A day in the life of the women of the palazzo went something like this: They brought in wood for the day from the storage area as well as the daily water supply, which came from a well, they baked bread, prepared meals, spun cloth, cut and sewed garments, tended to the sick, helped with the birth of children— and when all was said and done, they enjoyed a little conversation by the fire before repeating the same activities the next day. Paolo Certaldo, a writer of the time observed: "If you have womenfolk in the house, be sure they always have some task to do and are never idle, and if you have a young maid, put her to sew and not to read, as reading is no occupation for a woman unless she is to become a nun. Teach her all household duties; to make bread, to clean a capon, to make butter, to cook and do the laundry, to make a bed, to spin and to weave."

Whenever a place like Palazzo Davanzati transports me to another time, I have to catch myself and remember what life did not afford, and be grateful that I can romanticize at will what life could have been like in the past.

Fichi Ripieni Davanzati
Stuffed Figs Davanzati Style

SERVE 4

From the old manuscripts in its library, the recipe for stuffed figs from Palazzo Davanzati reads like this: "take large figs, the best you can find, take pears and nuts and apples and pound them together with bread crumbs and spices and sugar. Put the paste inside the figs and fold the leaves of the figs over the top. Fry the figs in oil and sprinkle the tops with sugar." Here is my adaptation of the recipe.

Butter a 9-inch casserole or Pyrex-type dish and set aside.

Preheat the oven to 350°F.

In a small bowl mix together the apple, pear, nuts, bread crumbs, sugar, cinnamon, ginger, and salt.

Place the figs cut side up in a single layer in the baking dish.

Divide and spoon the filling on top of each fig half. Pour the melted butter evenly over the top and bake the figs for about 20 minutes, or until just heated through. Serve immediately.

1 small Golden Delicious apple, peeled and grated

1 small pear, diced

2 tablespoons minced almonds or pine nuts

1 tablespoon fresh bread crumbs

2 tablespoons sugar

¼ teaspoon ground cinnamon

⅛ teaspoon ginger

Pinch of salt

8 large, fresh green figs, washed and cut in half lengthwise

2 tablespoons melted unsalted butter

A Taste for Saltless Bread

Pane Toscano (Tuscan Bread)

Pane Annunziata (Nancy's Tuscan Bread)

Crostini Rossi
(Little Diced-Tomato-and-Herb Toasts)

Crostini Neri
(Little Black Toasts with Chicken Liver Spread)

Fantasia di Tonno all'Annunziata
(Nancy's Tuna and Olive Spread)

SOME PEOPLE will do anything for a loaf of good Tuscan bread, including me. Bright and early on a crisp, sun-drenched day, and just when I was really in the mood for it, I headed for Teverina, a small town tucked away in the Tiber valley.

Along the way I noticed a frail elderly woman appear from the wooded area along the roadside. She walked slowly with the aid of a cane, and carried a basket and an ancient-looking sickle tucked under her arm. I stopped to see if I could give her a lift. A quick glance into her basket told me that she had been foraging for wild fennel, dandelions, and mushrooms.

In Tuscany just about everyone hunts for mushrooms, and there is quite a little street market going on when they are in season. I asked about the plump ones in her basket and she became animated as she called them out by name. There was *brunetta,* probably because of its brownish look, and *ovoli,* egg-shaped and a brilliant orange color. My next question was how to prepare them. Thin sliced and drizzled with olive oil, and *basta!* I must have been overzealous in my questioning, because she offered to give me the whole basket! I thanked her but refused, knowing what an effort it must have been to find them. I said good-bye, remembering my date to make bread. As I drove away I could not help but think of what a good example she was of a way of life that was passing by, along with traditions that will pass away as well.

Finally, the twisted mountain road led me to where Nancy Harmon Jenkins, an American cookbook author, lives. We met years ago in Puglia while we were

Foraging for wild mushrooms along the road to Teverina.

both at a conference about bread and the other food products of the region. Nancy has called Italy home for over thirty years. Her house is tucked away among lush forested hills hugging Monte Maggio, and to get there I had to negotiate the car down her ski-slope of a driveway. She was waiting for me near her olive groves. And she was ready to make the bread. She'd already prepared the starter dough, or *biga,* a loose batterlike consistency of flour, water, and a pinch of yeast that is allowed to ferment. This gives added structure to the bread, improves its flavor, and gives it a nice crumb. She uses *grano tenero,* a soft wheat that gives the bread a brown color and a nutty taste. I couldn't wait to get started and in no time we were in aprons and ready for the day's occupation.

What makes Tuscan bread so special is that it is made without salt, and there are many stories surrounding why this is so. From a simple baking point of view, saltless bread stays fresh longer, since salt draws moisture out, making bread become stale quite quickly. From a historical or maybe even folkloric point of view, it seems that around the start of the Middle Ages, rather than pay a tax on salt the Tuscans simply went without it and did not miss it very much. Tuscans will argue that their saltless bread is just fine because of what goes with bread—their cheeses and cured meats are highly seasoned and they compliment each other. They also believe that bread is a blank canvas for other foods. It is essential for *fettunta,* which is grilled bread drizzled with extra-virgin olive oil; broken into pieces, it is a thickener in soups like *papa al pomodoro* (p. 204), or a slice of it is often the surprise at the bottom of a soup bowl. When it is stale it is moistened and mixed with raw vegetables for *panzanella* (p. 203), or it becomes part of the sauce for *capriolo* (venison, p. 122), and it is used as stuffing for meats and vegetables.

As Nancy and I knead the dough we both regret that the art of bread making at home has all but disappeared today, not only in Tuscany but in many other regions of Italy. Women used to make the dough and bring it to a communal *forno* (oven) to be baked because the cost of fuel was so high. Today's women are in the workforce with little time for making bread, and bakeries are common and accessible, making *pane casareccio* (homemade bread) a thing of the past. We shape the dough into elongated loaves known as *filone*. Over a glass of homemade wine we wait for them to rise, then bake them to a golden-brown color. The smell is divine. Finally we open the oven door and the glory of crusty loaves is before us. Neither of us can wait for them to cool, so we cut into a loaf with a sharp knife, shattering the crisp crust. Hot steam rises from the loaf and warms our faces. *Quick, get the olive oil!* We drizzle the bread with Nancy's own oil and savor every bite.

For me, making bread is meditative as I get into the concentration and rhythm of kneading dough into a silky, smooth ball. No matter how many times I have done this I am in awe when I stop to think that making bread is a handmade miracle wheedled from soil, water, and air. Bread is necessary, comforting, and versatile. It truly deserves the phrase "staff of life," saltless or otherwise.

Pane Toscano
Tuscan Bread

MAKES 1 ROUND OR ELONGATED LOAF

MOTHER DOUGH

½ teaspoon active
dry yeast

½ cup warm water
(110°F)

¾ cup unbleached all-
purpose flour

SECOND DOUGH

1 teaspoon active
dry yeast

1¼ cups warm water
(110°F)

3 cups unbleached
all-purpose flour

2 tablespoons crushed ice

Cornmeal

Tuscan bread can be round or elongated into a shape known as a filone. *It is perfect in soups, and toasted or grilled for the classic antipasto known as* crostini. *This bread is best when made in a stand mixer, because a lot of air can be beaten into the dough, which will result in a crumb with lots of holes. Begin early in the day by making the "mother dough" first. This is the starter dough that will help give added strength to the finished dough before it goes into the oven. Try not to use too much flour or a heavy, tight crumb will result. I add crushed ice to produce a more open crumb. The dough will be tacky and very fluffy when it is risen.*

FOR THE MOTHER DOUGH

In a bowl, dissolve the yeast in the warm water then mix in the flour until a loose dough is formed. Cover and let rise for at least 3 hours at room temperature.

FOR THE SECOND DOUGH

Dissolve the yeast in the water in a stand mixer, and allow it to proof or get chalky-looking. Stir in all of the mother dough and begin adding the flour 1 cup at a time and beating it until a ball of dough is created that winds around the paddle. Add the crushed ice and continue beating for 5 minutes. The dough will look like shiny taffy.

Turn the dough out onto a floured surface and knead it for several minutes. Use a dough scraper to help move and turn the dough, as it will be sticky. Resist the temptation to add more flour—it will result in a tight-textured loaf.

Use the dough scraper to help lift the dough from the work surface to an oiled bowl. Cover the bowl tightly with plastic wrap and allow it to rise for at least 2 hours, or until it is doubled in size.

Preheat the oven to 450°F.

Punch down the dough with your fists and transfer it to a lightly floured work surface. Use the dough scraper to help knead and shape the dough into a round or an oval loaf. Place the dough on a wooden peel lined with a piece of parchment paper, or on a lightly greased baking sheet sprinkled with a bed of cornmeal. Allow it to rise covered for 45 minutes or until almost doubled in size.

Dust the top of the dough lightly with flour. Make several ½-inch slashes across the top of the loaf with a clean razor or a French lame, a tool used to slash bread before baking. This will prevent the dough from splitting at its sides as it bakes. Bake the bread for 20 minutes, then reduce the heat to 400°F and bake until the dough is nicely browned and sounds hollow when tapped.

Cool completely.

NOTE: If you make a lot of bread, invest in a baking stone. Your loaves will have a wonderful crusty texture, and the stone is great for pizza and focaccia, too. When using a stone, preheat the oven for at least 30 minutes before baking.

Pane Annunziata
Nancy's Tuscan Bread

MAKES 2 LOAVES

1 teaspoon active dry yeast

4 cups warm water (110°F)

9 cups unbleached all-purpose flour

1 cup whole wheat flour

1 teaspoon extra-virgin olive oil

Semolina or cornmeal to flour the work board

Nancy Harmon Jenkins makes Tuscan bread the traditional way, without salt. She begins two days prior to baking the bread by making a slurry, a loose starter dough that will help give texture, taste, and a nice rise to the final dough. This method is time-consuming—it takes three days—but it is well worth it to achieve a nearly authentic loaf. For a quicker version of Tuscan bread, see p. 94.

For the Slurry

Combine the yeast and ½ cup of water in a bowl, stir, and set aside.

Measure 2 cups of the unbleached flour into a large bowl. Make a hole in the center of the flour with your hands and pour in the yeast mixture. Move the flour from the sides of the bowl into the yeast mixture and combine. Gradually pour in 1 cup of water. Use a wooden spoon to mix the flour and yeast mixture together to form a thick slurry. Sprinkle another cup of the unbleached flour over the top of the slurry; cover the bowl with plastic wrap and set aside in a cool place to rise for 6 to 8 hours or overnight.

The next day add the whole wheat flour, 1 cup of warm water, and another cup of the unbleached all-purpose flour to the bowl with the slurry and mix, kneading the dough slightly in the bowl with your hands. The dough will be very sticky. Cover and set aside again to rise for 6 to 8 hours or overnight.

The next day stir in the 1½ cups of the remaining water. Work in the remaining flour, leaving a little of it aside to spread on the board or work surface.

Turn the dough onto the floured surface and knead it for 10 to

15 minutes, or until the dough is silky and springy and has lost its stickiness.

Place the dough in a large bowl sprayed with olive oil. Cover tightly with plastic wrap and place the dough in a warm place (75°F) to rise for 2 to 3 hours.

It is best to bake the dough on a baking stone or tiles. To do this preheat the oven stone at 450°F for 30 minutes prior to baking the bread.

Turn the risen dough out onto a lightly floured work surface, punch it down, knead it briefly, and form it into two big oval or round loaves. Set the loaves on 2 oven peels lined with cornmeal. Cover the loaves with a clean towel and allow them to rise for 45 minutes while the oven is heating.

Transfer the loaves from the peel to the stone; if you have only one peel, form one at a time.

Bake 10 minutes, then lower the heat to 350°F and continue baking another 40 to 45 minutes, or until the bread is nicely browned and sounds hollow when tapped with your knuckles.

To bake the loaves without a stone, form the loaves as above and place each one on a lightly oiled and cornmeal-lined baking sheet. Cover as above and let rise for 45 minutes. Bake in a preheated 375°F oven for 35–40 minutes, or until nicely browned.

Cool the bread on a rack before slicing.

NOTE: Traditionally, Tuscan bread is not slashed with a lame or razor before baking to allow steam to escape, but it is a good idea to do so, to prevent the bread from splitting as it bakes.

Crostini Rossi
Little Diced-Tomato-and-Herb Toasts

SERVES 4

3 large plum tomatoes, diced

1 clove garlic, minced

2 basil leaves, minced

3 sprigs flat-leaf Italian parsley, minced

2 tablespoons extra-virgin olive oil

¼ teaspoon fine sea salt

8 small slices toasted bread

I love the way Nancy describes the little toasts—crostini rossi (red toasts) and crostini neri *(black toasts)—that start off a Tuscan meal.* Crostini rossi *can only mean a tomato-salad topping for Tuscan bread, and the best is made with summer-ripe plum tomatoes.*

Mix the tomatoes, garlic, basil, parsley, olive oil, and salt in a bowl. Allow the mixture to marinate for several hours at room temperature.

Place two slices of bread on each of 4 salad plates. Divide and top the bread with the tomato mixture. Serve.

Crostini Neri
Little Black Toasts with Chicken Liver Spread

SERVES 6 AS AN ANTIPASTO

For crostini neri *(little black toasts), Nancy makes a chicken liver spread; this is the most classic Tuscan topping for* crostini.

Pick over the chicken livers, cutting away any green spots and removing any tough bits of fiber. Rinse gently and briefly in a colander and set aside to drain.

Heat the olive oil over medium-low heat in a sauté pan, and when it is hot stir in the onions, garlic, and half the parsley and cook gently until the onion is soft and pale yellow, about 10 minutes. Stir in the anchovies and use a fork to mash them into the other ingredients.

Pat the chicken livers dry with paper towels. Raise the heat to medium, push the vegetable mixture to one side, and add the livers in the center of the pan. Cook, tossing the livers to brown quickly. As they cook, chop them coarsely with a wooden spoon. After they have changed color from rosy to brown, stir in the wine and broth. Lower the heat to medium-low and cook, stirring occasionally for about 15 minutes, or until the livers are uniform in color and most of the liquid has been absorbed. As the livers cook, continue to break them up with a fork or spoon until they form a coarse paste, which is traditional; but if you prefer a smoother texture, process the mixture in a food processor. Stir in the capers and remaining parsley along with the lemon juice and mix well. Taste and add salt if necessary along with lots of black pepper, and more lemon juice if desired.

Spread the liver mixture on the bread slices and place them on a serving platter. Serve warm or at room temperature.

½ pound chicken livers

2 tablespoons extra-virgin olive oil

½ cup onion, minced

1 small garlic clove, minced

2 tablespoons parsley, minced

2 anchovy fillets, coarsely chopped

½ cup dry Tuscan Vin Santo or dry white wine

2 tablespoons chicken broth, beef broth, or water

1 tablespoon salted capers, rinsed, drained, and chopped

Fresh-squeezed lemon juice to taste

Salt and coarse black pepper to taste

12 slices toasted bread

Fantasia di Tonno all'Annunziata
Nancy's Tuna and Olive Spread

SERVES 6 TO 8 AS AN ANTIPASTO

1 pound black or green
olives, pitted

½ cup capers in salt,
rinsed well and drained

1 small clove garlic,
coarsely chopped

Half a small (6⅛-ounce)
can tuna packed
in olive oil

½ cup extra-virgin
olive oil

Fresh lemon juice to taste

*T*his crostini, *topped with juicy black and green olives and com-bined with tuna and capers is* una fantasia *(a creation), as Nancy likes to call it. It is also good as a dip for raw vegetables. Be sure to use fresh olives, not canned.*

Combine all the ingredients except the lemon juice in a blender or food processor and process very briefly to make a coarse-textured paste. Taste and add a few drops of lemon juice.

Scoop the ingredients into a bowl and serve with toasted bread or with raw vegetables.

The tuna mixture may be prepared up to a week in advance and refrigerated in a jar with a thin layer of olive oil over the top. Bring to room temperature before serving.

A House with a View

I had not seen the house in Cortona since renting it nearly seven years ago for a month's vacation. And I never expected that the house would eventually become famous, thanks to a book written about it, describing what it was like for an American to buy and renovate it. It was just a country house set high on a hillside that overlooked the lush Val di Chiana, with the added bonus that you could see one of Italy's largest lakes, Lago Trasimeno, near Perugia in the distance, a lake made famous by the fact that Hannibal defeated the Romans there in 217 B.C. But I wanted to see it again, if only from a distance, so, after filming the making of Tuscan bread I asked the crew if they would mind if we stopped in Cortona.

As soon as I saw the sign for Torreone, I knew we were close to the *strada bianca* (dirt road) leading to the house. The shady, narrow road lined on either side with towering ancient trees was just as I remembered it, and I recalled as we approached the house how each day I would walk this road so that I could look over the valley and admire the neat landscape below, where puffs of white smoke spewed gently from the chimneys of stone farmhouses that appeared in the distance, charmingly nestled among cypress, chestnut, and olive trees. My train of thought was suddenly broken and there it was, the house that I cooked in, slept in, read in, and entertained in, still as I remembered it, with its rosy, peach-colored stone exterior accented with chocolate-brown shutters. But it looked grander now, more finished. There was more landscaping, more roses and flowering shrubs than the geraniums that I remembered in terra-cotta pots, and the balcony was overflowing with bougainvillea.

I had a great urge to walk up the steep steps and knock on the door to let the present owners know how much I enjoyed my stay here. The house is known as *Bramasole,* which means "to yearn for the sun," and I yearned to be inside those walls again, but something made me hesitate, and I stood by the roadside and pointed out to the crew the floor plan of the house as I knew it. I wondered how much had changed inside, and I knew it had, since its owner, a well-known author, had written the book about the house and how she came to buy and restore it. Of course there were changes, but I preferred to remember it when I lived in it; my room with whitewashed walls had a balcony. Over the window were whimsically painted gold stars that made me smile when I went to sleep at night, and the brownish colored terra-cotta floor was so cool that I gave up walking around in my bare feet.

I pointed out where the kitchen was, and the sweet country dining room with the hand-painted but badly damaged scenes on the wall. Perhaps they had restored it? I entertained lots of American friends at the country dining room table with the simple credenza at one end that held all kinds of ceramic ware. And I recalled my Italian friends from Reggio Emilia and Florence coming for a day visit. I remembered the peach cobbler that I made with the *pesche bianche* that I bought in the market in Cortona on Via Dardano, and how amazed they were at this unfamiliar way to use white peaches. And I laughed when I recalled the night that I grilled calamari and porcini mushrooms, except that I had let the mushrooms sit too long in the *limonaia* (storage area), and they were full of worms when I went to retrieve them for the evening meal!

If there was just one tense moment at *Bramasole,* it was the night of my arrival after a long travel day from the States, when I finally put head to pillow for the night—only to be awakened from a sound sleep in the early morning hours by the local police pounding on the door and raining flashlights all over the place! It seems the owners forgot to tell the local authorities that they had rented the house to me for a month. But after some explaining in my sleepy Italian all was well and they bid me *buona notte.*

Even though we could not go into the house, we could walk from it on the preserved old Roman road leading from *Bramasole* to the Piazza Garabaldi. The walk takes you right into town along terraced hillsides with breathtaking views. So, with the crew and camera gear in hand, we made our way, stepping over the ancient stones and discovering wild fennel, blackberries, rose hips, and elderberries, and I reminisced about the daily trips I made over this road to buy fruit and vegetables at the market, and to stop at the *pasticerria* for fresh bread and biscotti. It always seemed that I had more groceries than I could possibly use, but being in Italy does that to you; it makes you want to experience everything at once.

The crew seemed glad that we had taken this little detour, and as we continued on I glanced back for one last look at *Bramasole* as it slipped from view, and mused to myself that it deserved to have a book written about it.

Maria Pia's Pleasing Paté

Paté di Tonno alla Maria Pia
(Maria Pia's Tuna Paté)

Cacciucco alla Livornese
(Classic Fish Stew from Livorno)

Insalata di Tonno, Patate, e Capperi
(Tuna, Potato, and Caper Salad)

Pomodori Ripieni con Tonno
(Tomatoes Stuffed with Tuna)

Triglia in Umido (Stewed Red Mullet)

A CAN OF TUNA stashed on the pantry shelf does not evoke "gourmet food" in the minds of many, but when my friend Maria Pia announced that she was going to transform it very quickly into a pleasing fashion-plate paté, I knew she could work a culinary miracle. After all, here was a woman who also turned carriage stalls for horses into her elegant Tuscan home.

Maria Pia lives in Campo, a small town not too far from the Campo dei Miracoli, which is the main Piazza, famous for its flamboyant twelfth-century *duomo* (cathedral) with its intricately carved flowers, animals, and patterns. The piazza also contains the Leaning Tower of Pisa, which I never tire of seeing. I love to come for long visits, and I even have my own room at Maria Pia's house. I always smile when I pass by her son Michele's room filled with Americana including empty Coca-Cola cans, Michael Jordan posters, and United States flag.

Since Pisa is close to the Ligurian Sea, it makes sense that Maria Pia likes to make fish dishes. One of her favorite recipes is a tuna paté that she serves when the weather is hot, accompanying it with a mixed green salad, or fresh peas cooked in olive oil, and flavored with onions. Only very good tuna packed in olive oil must be used, she cautioned as she opened a large can. I must admit, the naked contents dumped into a bowl didn't exactly tingle my taste buds, but I was optimistic waiting to see what came next. From the stove top Maria Pia took boiled potatoes and mashed them into a buttery mound, then combined them with the tuna. At this point it still didn't look like much of anything, until she very quickly fashioned a fish shape out of the mixture, centered on a pretty platter.

Maria Pia makes triglia in umido, *a delicious and quick-to-prepare red mullet dish.*

But this "fish out of water" wasn't ready to eat just yet. Maria Pia likes to give it a coating of homemade mayonnaise. She combined egg yolks, olive oil, lemon juice, and a pinch of salt, and whirled everything in a food processor. As she covered the paté with the sunny, yellow velvet coating it began to take on the look of immediate temptation. To complete the dish, a couple of capers became fish eyes, and a sprig of parsley added a whimsical touch when inserted into the mouth.

This was just the beginning, she announced like a schoolteacher emphasizing a point. She removed a dish holding fish from the refrigerator and proceeded to give a detailed explanation of *triglia* (red mullet), a delicate, tiny, and bony saltwater fish that lives up to its name with its orange-red skin, and that comes from the seaside area of Livorno, southwest of Pisa. Great care must be taken to handle and cook the fish slowly so that it does not break apart. The classic way to do this is *in umido,* or stewed, with tomatoes, parsley, and some red pepper flakes for spiciness (p. 113). It is served with boiled potatoes, or *cippoline,* small white onions. And the best part is that it can be ready in minutes. I was offered a taste. The *triglia* was delicious—moist and flavorful without being too heady. That is the sign of a good cook, like Maria Pia, someone who knows how to balance ingredients, when to add flavor, and when to refrain from too much of a good thing.

The paté did not disappoint, either, and with such a rich taste that lingers in your mouth, it was hard to think of this as just canned tuna and potatoes!

I was taught a great lesson that day: Never take a can of tuna for granted again. Oh, the possibilities! *Bravissima,* Maria Pia!

Petti di Pollo al Vino Bianco (Chicken Breasts with White Wine Sauce), page 24

Bistecca alla Fiorentina (Grilled T-Bone Steak), page 40

Cacciucco alla Livornese (Classic Fish Stew from Livorno), page 110

Buccellato di Lucca
(Raisin-Anise Bread),
page 66

Schiacciata con l'uva
(Grape Harvest
Bread), page 124

Mele con la Salsa di Lampone (Apples with Raspberry Sauce), page 140

Gnocchi di Spinachi e Ricotta (Spinach and Ricotta Cheese Gnocchi), page 150

Pappardelle con la Salsa di Funghi Misti
(Wide Noodles with Mixed Mushroom Sauce), page 159

Panforte (Fruitcake), page 170

Ricciarelli di Siena (Siena-Style Almond Cookies), page 178

Pappa al Pomodoro (Tomato Bread Soup), page 204

Scarola e Fagioli (Escarole and Beans), page 207

Paté di Tonno alla Maria Pia
Maria Pia's Tuna Paté

As Maria Pia says, *"You must use the best tuna in olive oil,"* but *a good store-bought mayonnaise may be substituted for home-made.*

In a food processor or blender whirl together the egg yolks, egg, mustard, salt, pepper, and lemon or lime juice until smooth. Dribble in the olive oil through the feed tube with the motor running until the mixture has a mayonnaise consistency.

Store the mayonnaise in a jar in the refrigerator for up to 5 days.

Puree the potatoes with the tuna, capers (Reserving 2 for the eyes), and sea salt.

On a serving platter form the tuna mixture into the shape of a fish with your hands. Frost the fish with the mayonnaise and insert the reserved capers for the eyes.

Maria Pia serves the paté with a green salad or fresh peas and onions cooked in olive oil. It is also good accompanied with thin slices of grilled bread.

VARIATION: Use thin slices of cucumbers to create fish scales over the mayonnaise.

NOTE: Lining a fish mold with plastic wrap and packing it with the paté mixture is another technique to getting the "fish" look for this recipe. Simply remove the plastic wrap carefully after inverting the mold onto a serving dish.

TO MAKE THE MAYONNAISE

2 egg yolks

1 large egg

1¼ tablespoons Dijon-type mustard

Pinch salt

Coarse black pepper to taste

3 tablespoons lemon or lime juice

1¾ cups extra-virgin olive oil

THE PATÉ

4 medium-size cooked potatoes, cooled and peeled, about 1¾ pounds

12-ounce can tuna packed in olive oil

2 tablespoons capers in salt, rinsed

Pinch sea salt

Cacciucco alla Livornese
Classic Fish Stew from Livorno

MAKES ABOUT 2 QUARTS OR 8 SERVINGS

1 large onion, peeled and coarsely chopped

3 cloves garlic, peeled

¼ cup parsley leaves

8 basil leaves

¼ cup olive oil

½ teaspoon hot red pepper flakes

⅔ cup dry white wine

2 cups plum tomatoes, peeled and diced

1 cup clam juice, fish bouillon, or water

½ teaspoon fine sea salt or more to taste

½ pound cleaned squid, cut into 1-inch rings

½ pound swordfish, skinned and cut into 1-inch chunks

½ pound medium shrimp (about 13), shelled

¼ pound sea scallops

¼ pound monkfish, cut into 1-inch pieces

2 tablespoons fresh lemon juice

8 toasted bread slices

This dish originated with fishermen in Livorno; they sold the best of their catch and used what was left over and unwanted at day's end to make fish stew. A variety of fish went into the pot, including squid, monk fish, and cod. Tradition dictates that at least five different types of fish be used, one for each of the Cs in the word cacciucco, *which means mixture. In this preparation start by adding the fish that takes the longest to cook. Make sure all the fish is cut the same size for even cooking. From start to finish the stew should take about 25 minutes and is even better the next day. Crackling, crusty bread and a crisp salad make the meal both wholesome and complete. This stew is usually cooked in an earthenware pot atop the stove. Use your heaviest pot.*

In a food processor or by hand, mince the onion, garlic, parsley, and basil together. Heat the oil in a heavy-duty pot and stir in the minced onion mixture. Cook over low heat until the ingredients soften, then stir in the pepper flakes and cook 1 minute longer.

Raise the heat to high, pour in the wine, and allow most of it to evaporate. Lower the heat and stir in the tomatoes, clam juice, and salt. When bubbles just begin to appear on the sides of the pot, begin adding the fish pieces in the order given, allowing the squid to cook for 5 minutes before adding the swordfish. Cook just until the fish turns opaque or whitish and flakes easily with a fork and the shrimp have turned pink. Stir in the lemon juice and correct the salt if necessary.

Ladle the soup over the bread slices and serve piping hot.

Insalata di Tonno, Patate, e Capperi
Tuna, Potato, and Caper Salad

SERVES 8

Tuna packed in olive oil is used in many inventive ways in the Tuscan kitchen. I enjoy the challenge of bringing canned tuna to new heights in my own kitchen, too, so I offer this delicious and easy-to-prepare tuna, potato, and caper salad that is perfect for hot weather. It is best to make it several hours ahead of time to allow the flavors to mingle. Mound it on a nice platter, or make individual molds using new PVC piping or another type of cylindrical form, like aluminum molds, to create an eye-catching presentation.

Boil the potatoes until a knife is easily inserted. Drain and allow them to cool. Peel the potatoes, dice them, and put them in a large bowl.

Put the shallots or onions in a small saucepan, stir in the vinegar, and bring the mixture to a boil. Lower the heat and simmer the shallots until they have softened and all the vinegar has evaporated. Transfer the shallots to a small bowl and allow them to cool.

Add the shallots or onions, tuna, capers, parsley, tarragon, celery salt, pepper, and salt to the potatoes. Mix gently to combine the ingredients well. Add the olive oil and mix again.

Transfer the mixture to a platter and garnish with cherry tomatoes. Serve at room temperature.

NOTE: For an elegant molded presentation divide and pack the mixture into 8 or 9 new 3 × 2-inch PVC piping sections. Carefully place each on an individual salad plate lined with arugula or other salad leaves. Lift the piping off and garnish each plate with cherry tomatoes.

4 large all-purpose potatoes (about 1¾ pounds), scrubbed

½ cup finely minced shallots or onions

¼ cup white wine vinegar

Two 6-ounce cans tuna in olive oil

⅓ cup capers in salt, rinsed, dried, and minced

4 tablespoons minced parsley

4 tablespoons minced tarragon

1¼ teaspoons celery salt

Coarse black pepper to taste

Fine sea salt to taste

¼ cup extra-virgin olive oil

Cherry tomatoes for garnish

Pomodori Ripieni con Tonno
Tomatoes Stuffed with Tuna

SERVES 4

4 beefsteak or large tomatoes with stem tops

Fine sea salt to taste

1 six-ounce can tuna in olive oil, drained and flaked

1 tablespoon capers in salt, rinsed, drained, and dried

1 shallot or small onion, diced

2 tablespoons minced parsley

2 tablespoons minced tarragon

4 tablespoons prepared or homemade mayonnaise (p. 109)

Coarse black pepper to taste

When Maria Pia comes to visit me I know it is best to carry on the tuna theme in my kitchen. I take the biggest tomatoes I can harvest from my garden and fill them with canned tuna and herbs. They look attractive and are perfect with crusty bread and fruit for an al fresco *lunch.*

Leaving the stem on, cut ¼ inch off the top of each tomato and reserve.

Squeeze each tomato gently with your hands to remove the seeds. Use a small spoon to remove some of the pulp, which can be saved to use in soup.

Salt the interior of each tomato lightly and set aside to drain upside down on paper towels for about 20 minutes.

Meanwhile, combine the remaining ingredients in a bowl. Stuff each tomato with some of the filling. Replace the stem tops and place each one on serving plates.

VARIATION: Add ½ cup cooked chickpeas or *cannellini* beans to the filling for added protein and fiber.

Triglia in Umido
Stewed Red Mullet

SERVES 2 TO 3

Triglia in Umido *(stewed red mullet) is another fish dish that comes from Livorno, and one that Maria Pia loves to serve to company. It is quick to prepare and ready in 15 minutes. Red mullet is extremely delicate, so cooking it slowly is the key to keeping it in one piece.*

Heat the olive oil in a sauté pan large enough to hold the fish in a single layer over medium heat. When the oil begins to shimmer stir in the garlic and swirl in the oil until it begins to brown. Stir in the red pepper flakes and cook for 1 minute. Stir in the parsley, chives, and tomatoes. Lower the heat and simmer the mixture for 10 minutes uncovered. Place the fish on top and spoon some of the sauce over it. Cook for about 5 minutes, turning them once with a wide-face spatula. The fish is cooked when it flakes easily when poked with a fork. Add salt and pepper to taste.

Serve the fish with some of the sauce and boiled tiny new potatoes or boiled onions.

2 tablespoons extra-virgin olive oil

2 whole cloves garlic, peeled

1 teaspoon hot red pepper flakes

1 tablespoon minced parsley

1 tablespoon minced chives

1 pound fresh or canned crushed tomatoes

1 pound fresh, whole gutted red mullet, about 4 to 5 fish, rinsed and dried

Fine sea salt to taste

Coarse black pepper to taste

Vineyard Kitchen

Pinci (Thick Noodles)

La Salsa di Briciola
(Little Cubed Bread Sauce)

Capriolo Scottiglia
(Venison Stew Cooked in Red Wine)

Spezzatino Toscano (Tuscan Beef Stew)

Schiacciata con l'uva
(Grape Harvest Bread)

Torta di Mele (Apple Cake)

Anelli di Mele (Fried Apple Rings)

Torta di Riso (Rice Cake)

MARIA GORELLI IS a quiet, petite chef who works at Villa Banfi Vineyards, in a very modern kitchen that overlooks the beautiful views of Montalcino in central Tuscany. The town of Montalcino is all about serious wine production, as evidenced by the miles and miles of vineyards; Villa Banfi has over seven thousand acres under cultivation.

My mission that day was to cook typical Tuscan dishes with Maria in the estate kitchen. Maria, also known by her friends and coworkers as "Santa Maria Gorelli" because of her quiet demeanor, used to own a restaurant that served fifty, but gave it up to cook here. She has definite ideas about how things should be done in the kitchen and is well-equipped with traits that I admire in a chef — imaginative thinking in blending flavors, making the most of what is in season, and an ability to think on her feet in a demanding environment, where she cooks for guests of the estate each day. Most of all, Maria never sways from the principles of authentic Tuscan preparation.

One of her great disappointments is that young people today do not know how to cook, and she fears that a lot of traditional foods will soon disappear, giving way to fast food.

My role was Maria's helper as she demonstrated how to make *pinci* (p. 119), a typical thick spaghetti as long as a shoelace. The soft dough was rolled out with a rolling pin into a flat sheet, then cut into strips. It looked doable, until Maria anchored the end of each strip with one hand and rolled it out into a plump, round strand with the other hand until it was about nine inches long. As

Maria Gorelli makes pinci, *the typical pasta of the region.*

she made them they cascaded onto a bed of semolina flour; this was to prevent them from sticking. Maria then loosely coiled them around her hand and set them aside while the water boiled.

Next, there was the proper sauce to consider for the *pinci,* and for Maria that meant *La Salsa di Briciola,* (p. 121), literally a sauce made from small cubes of stale bread. Maria cut the bread into miniature cubes and with a few peppercorns and some olive oil made a sauce for the *pinci* in about two minutes. When this was ready, the *pinci* was cooked, drained, and tossed with the sauce. A few diced tomatoes and basil leaves for garnish added the right visual touch.

Later, outside in the courtyard, a beautiful table with an arrangement of sunflowers, cherry tomatoes *(ciliegini)* still clinging to their stems, and brilliant red and yellow peppers was set against a backdrop of stone walls and brick archways. Maria and I were seated in front of the dishes she created for our television audience, *pinci* with the *salsa di briciole*, and *capriolo scottiglia* (p. 122). To my taste buds, they reflected Tuscan country cooking at its best. With a glass of Centine, another labor of love straight from the vineyards, I toasted Maria for her dedication to preserving the foods of Tuscany. *"Cin cin!"*

Pinci
Thick Noodles

SERVES 5–6

Tasting pinci, *a thick type of spaghetti, is a good enough reason to visit the wine country of Montalcino. And chef Maria Gorelli turns them out by hand faster than any machine can in the Castello Banfi kitchen. In other parts of Tuscany these delicious noodles are called* pici, *which just goes to show how localized the cuisine of Tuscany can be. Make the dough in a food processor or by hand. If you do not want to make them from scratch, substitute* bucatini, *a thicker (and hollow) cut of dried pasta found in grocery stores.*

2½ cups unbleached all-purpose flour

½ cup semolina flour

⅛ teaspoon fine sea salt

1 large egg, slightly beaten

Warm water as needed

To make the dough by hand heap the flours with the salt on a work surface and mix them together with your hands. Make a hole in the center of the flour and add the egg; begin mixing the flour from the inside of the wall into the egg. When you have a rough mass, push the excess flour out of the way and knead the dough into a smooth ball. If the mixture seems dry as you form the dough, add 1 tablespoon of water at a time until you have the right consistency. Cover the dough with a bowl and allow it to rest for 30 minutes to relax the gluten.

If using a food processor, place all the flour and salt in the bowl of the processor and whirl to blend. Add the egg and water if needed through the feed tube. Process until a ball forms around the blade. Remove and cover the dough as directed above.

To form the *pinci,* divide the dough in half; work with one half at a time and keep the rest covered. On a floured surface, use a rolling pin to roll the dough out into a rectangle the thickness of pizza dough, about ⅛ inch. Cut 9 × ¼-inch-wide strips from the dough. Anchor one end of each strip with one hand, and with the other roll and stretch each one under your palm, creating a thick strand. Coil each one loosely around your hand, forming a "nest," and place them on a towel sprinkled with semolina.

To cook, bring 4 quarts of water to a boil. Add 1 tablespoon of sea salt and 1 teaspoon of olive oil. Lift the *pinci* from the towel and drop into the water. Cook until al dente. This will be a little chewier than regular spaghetti because of its thickness. Drain and toss the *pinci* with *Salsa di Briciola* (p. 121).

La Salsa di Briciola
Little Cubed Bread Sauce

MAKES 2 CUPS

*S*tale bread has new meaning in this sauce for pinci (p. 119) or any other pasta. Use bread that has a coarse crumb so that it will hold its shape. La salsa di briciola, *literally a sauce made with bits of morsels of bread, exemplifies* cucina povera, *simple country cooking where the ingenuity of the cook and the lesson of "waste not want not" hold firm in the Tuscan kitchen.*

Pour the olive oil into a sauté pan large enough to hold the bread cubes in a single layer. Add the hot pepper and swirl in the oil, pressing on them with a wooden spoon. Stir in the garlic and cook until it softens but does not brown. Stir in the bread cubes and coat them in the oil but do not brown them; they should remain light golden. Stir in the salt and keep the sauce warm while the *pinci* is cooking.

   Drain the *pinci,* transfer it to a large platter, and pour the sauce over the top. Toss gently to coat all the strands with the sauce. Sprinkle the tomatoes over the top and garnish with the basil leaves. Serve hot.

1¾ cups extra-virgin olive oil

1 small hot red pepper, broken into pieces

1 tablespoon minced garlic

1¾ cups very small-cubed, stale bread

½ teaspoon fine sea salt

½ cup chopped cherry tomatoes

2 whole basil leaves

Capriolo Scottiglia
Venison Stew Cooked in Red Wine

SERVES 6 TO 8

3½ pounds deer meat, leg cut, in 1-inch pieces

5 cups dry red wine (such as Centine)

Olive oil

3 ribs celery, cut into 1-inch chunks

1 medium red onion, peeled and quartered

2 large cloves garlic, peeled

2 tablespoons fresh rosemary needles

8 or 9 fresh sage leaves

1 teaspoon or more of fine sea salt

Coarse black pepper to taste

3 cups pureed tomatoes

Tuscany has strict rules when it comes to hunting. Wild boar may be hunted with a license, but deer are off-limits; you must buy it from a butcher. One of the typical dishes derived from hunters is capriolo scottiglia, *deer meat cooked in wine.* Scottiglia *means to be burned, and in this case it means that the meat must be well browned before the wine is added. Marinating the meat in wine overnight will help to give the dish a rich taste. It is best to use the leg cut of meat, which will need to cook for three hours, so start the process early in the day. Stew beef can be substituted for deer.*

The day before making the stew, marinate the meat in 3 cups of the wine.

When ready to cook, drain off the wine and reserve it. Dry the meat on paper towels and set aside.

In a large cast-iron or heavy-duty stove-top skillet, brown the meat in the olive oil over medium-high heat. If your skillet is small, do this in batches. Do not pile the meat pieces on top of each other or they will not brown evenly.

Meanwhile, mince the celery, onion, garlic, rosemary, and sage together until fine. I do this in a food processor.

When all the meat is browned add the minced vegetables to the skillet and cook until the vegetables begin to soften. Add salt and pepper and 2 cups of the reserved wine. Raise the heat to high and allow half of the wine to evaporate. Lower the heat to a simmer, add the tomatoes and cook for 2 or 3 minutes. Cover the skillet and cook the meat over low heat for about 3 hours, or until fork tender.

Spezzatino Toscano
Tuscan Beef Stew

SERVES 4 TO 6

*T*he word spezzatino, *meaning "little broken pieces," also refers to stew, and this is one that I like to prepare at home. Like Maria Gorelli's* scottiglia *(p. 122) it uses red wine, which produces a rich flavor. It is a great company dish that can be made ahead of time and tastes better two days later. Remember that the success of any stewed meat dish is to cook it slowly in a heavy-duty pot.*

Heat the olive oil in an earthenware or other heavy-duty pot and cook the pancetta over medium-high heat until it begins to brown. Stir in the meat and brown it. Sprinkle with the salt and pepper. Stir in the onion, garlic, basil, sage, and rosemary and continue cooking until the onions soften.

In a small bowl combine the wine and tomatoes and slowly pour the mixture into the pot. Lower the heat, cover the pot, and simmer the meat for at least 45 minutes, or until it is fork-tender.

Stir in the peas.

Place a slice of bread in each individual soup bowl and ladle the stew over the bread.

2 tablespoons extra-virgin olive oil

¼ pound pancetta, diced

2 pounds stew beef, cut into 1-inch pieces and well dried with paper towels

1 teaspoon fine sea salt

Coarse black pepper to taste

1 large onion, peeled and thinly sliced

2 cloves garlic, cut into thin slices

4 or 5 basil leaves

3 sage leaves

1 large sprig rosemary

1½ cups red wine (Centine or Chianti)

1¼ pounds plum tomatoes, chopped

2 cups fresh or frozen peas

Slices of toasted stale bread

Schiacciata con l'uva
Grape Harvest Bread

MAKES 1 LARGE, RECTANGULAR FLAT BREAD

1 teaspoon active dried yeast

1 cup warm water (110°F)

6 tablespoons sugar

5½ tablespoons extra-virgin olive oil

2½ to 2¾ cups unbleached all-purpose flour

1 teaspoon salt

2 tablespoons rosemary needles, finely minced

2½ cups red seedless grapes, stemmed, washed, and dried

1 large egg, slightly beaten

Walking through the miles and miles of vineyards at Castello Banfi is meditative. From the back of the castello, Monte Sant'Amiata, a now-defunct volcano, casts a looming presence over the sloping vines. When it is vendemmia *(harvest season), the grapes will be plucked and carried away on huge trucks to the winery. There they begin their slow transformation into wine. Grapes that are not good enough for the crush are good enough for* schiacciata con l'uva, *a sweet, flat yeast bread embedded with grapes.*

Dissolve the yeast in the water in a large bowl and let sit for 5 minutes. Stir in 2 tablespoons of the sugar and 2 tablespoons of the olive oil.

In a small bowl mix 2½ cups of flour with the salt and add it to the yeast mixture. Work the ingredients with your hands until a ball of dough forms. Add additional flour as needed, but do not make the dough too stiff. Knead the dough for about 5 minutes, or until it is smooth.

Grease a large bowl with ½ teaspoon of the olive oil and turn the dough in it. Cover the bowl tightly with plastic wrap and place it in a warm place to rise until doubled, about 1 hour.

Brush a 17½ × 11¼-inch baking sheet with 1 teaspoon of the olive oil. Place a piece of parchment cut to fit in the bottom and set aside.

Preheat the oven to 375°F.

After the dough has risen, punch it down and turn it out onto a floured surface. Spread it out roughly with your hands and sprinkle the rosemary over the top. Fold the dough over the rosemary and knead it a few times to evenly distribute the rosemary. Use a rolling pin to roll the dough into a 20 × 16-inch rectangle. Place the dough in the pan, stretching it about 1 inch over the sides of the pan. Brush the dough with the remaining olive oil; scatter the grapes evenly over the top and press them into the dough with your hands. Sprinkle 2 tablespoons of the sugar over the grapes.

Bring the overhanging pieces of dough from the 2 longest sides toward the middle and pinch the seam together. Cut most of the excess dough off the 2 remaining short sides, leaving about ½ inch extending. Then fold the dough in on itself, pinching the ends closed. Use a fork to crimp the 2 short ends. The finished size should be about 15 by 8 inches.

Reroll the dough scraps and use them to make a decorative pattern on top. I use a small knife to cut leaves and vines, and then I use small balls of dough to make bunches of grapes.

Cover the dough and allow it to rise for 30 minutes. Brush the top with the beaten egg and sprinkle the top evenly with the remaining sugar.

Bake on the middle rack of the oven for 35 to 40 minutes, or until the dough is nicely browned on top and bottom.

Let the *schiacciata* cool for 30 minutes, then carefully lift it out with the parchment paper onto a wire rack. Let it cool to warm. Carefully pull the parchment paper away from the bottom, or leave it in place and remove after cutting the *schiacciata* into serving pieces. This is best served warm the day that it is made.

Torta di Mele
Apple Cake

SERVES 8

4 large eggs at room temperature

½ cup sugar

1 tablespoon vanilla extract

¼ cup heavy cream or sour cream

1 tablespoon grated lemon zest

¾ cup unbleached all-purpose flour

¾ teaspoon baking powder

Pinch salt

6 cups sliced Golden Delicious apples (about 4 or 5 large)

2 tablespoons warm apple jelly or apricot jam

Maria Gorelli was such a gracious host during the taping of Ciao Italia *that she even found time to make some typical Tuscan biscotti, which we all enjoyed after the filming. We talked about our favorite* dolci *and she was intrigued by my description of a moist apple cake that was a favorite of the renowned Tuscan chef Edgardo Sandoli, so I gave her the recipe. When I returned home, there was a letter from Maria telling me that* la torta è squisita! *This cake reminds me of apple pancakes; the batter is thin, there are more apples than batter, and the cake does not rise very high.*

Line an 8-inch square baking pan with aluminum foil, allowing enough for a 1-inch overhang. Butter and flour the foil and set the pan aside.

Preheat the oven to 350°F.

In a large bowl beat the eggs with the sugar with a handheld mixer until the mixture is fluffy and lemon colored. Beat in the vanilla and heavy or sour cream. Stir in the lemon zest.

On a sheet of waxed paper sift the flour, baking powder, and salt together. Beat the flour mixture into the egg mixture on medium speed. Fold in the apples.

Pour the batter into the foil-lined pan. Bake for 35 to 40 minutes, or until the apples are nicely browned.

Transfer the cake to a wire rack. Brush the top of the cake with the warm apple jelly or apricot jam. Let the cake cool to warm. Carefully lift the foil out of the pan. Remove the foil from the cake and discard. Serve the cake cut into squares.

NOTE: Why buy expensive pastry brushes to brush tarts and cakes? Instead buy small inexpensive paint brushes at the hardware store.

Anelli di Mele
Fried Apple Rings

SERVES 8

When I mentioned apple cake to Maria she was quick to remind me of another dessert that Tuscans love: fried apple rings dipped in a yeast batter made with white wine. They are a favorite at Carnivale time and are best eaten hot. These are traditionally deep-fried but I prefer to use less oil by frying them in a skillet with just enough oil to brown them sufficiently.

Dissolve the yeast in the warm water and allow it to stand for 5 minutes or until it looks chalky and bubbly. Whisk in the wine, sugar, egg, olive oil, and salt. Mix well. Whisk in the flour to make a smooth-looking batter. Cover and allow the mixture to rest for 1 hour at room temperature.

Dip the apple slices a few at a time in the batter, making sure they are well coated.

Heat ½ cup of the oil in a skillet and when it begins to shimmer add the apple slices a few at a time. Do not crowd them. Fry them until golden brown on each side.

When they are fried, transfer them to a baking sheet lined with paper towels to drain. Keep them warm in a low oven until all the slices have been fried. Add more oil to the pan as necessary.

Transfer the slices to a serving platter and sprinkle them with confectioner's sugar. Serve warm.

1 teaspoon active dried yeast

¼ cup warm water (110°F.)

½ cup dry white wine at room temperature

½ cup sugar

1 large egg

2 tablespoons extra-virgin olive oil

Pinch salt

1 cup unbleached all-purpose flour

3 large (about ¾ pound) Golden Delicious apples, cored and cut into ¼-inch-thick rounds

½ to ¾ cup vegetable oil for frying

Confectioner's sugar

Torta di Riso
Rice Cake

SERVES 8

½ cup raisins

¼ cup orange liqueur or rum

4 cups milk

¾ cup sugar

1½ cups arborio rice

Grated zest of 1 large lemon or orange

½ cup diced candied orange peel

½ cup slivered almonds

2 large eggs

¼ teaspoon salt

1 teaspoon cinnamon

½ cup heavy cream, mascarpone cheese, or plain yogurt

Being in the kitchen with Maria Gorelli brought back fond memories of the many times I have traveled to this timeless town devoted to wine. While there a few years ago I had the privilege of teaching a Tuscan cooking class with Italian rice expert Edgardo Sandoli. We were well suited to one another in the kitchen, and Edgardo made this wonderful torta di riso (rice cake) made with arborio rice for us to enjoy after we had sent the students home. The cake is easy to make and cooked in a bagnomaria, a water bath, to create even heat. Arborio rice is available in supermarkets and specialty stores; it is the same rice used to make risotto.

Butter and flour a 9- by- 2-inch cake pan. Line the bottom of the pan with a sheet of parchment paper and brush the top with melted butter. Set the pan aside.

Preheat the oven to 350°F.

Put the raisins in a small bowl, pour the liqueur over them and allow to marinate at least 30 minutes before making the cake.

Slowly bring the milk to a boil in a saucepan, lower the heat, and stir in the sugar and the rice. Lower heat to simmer, cover the pan and allow the rice to cook until all the milk is absorbed, about 25 to 30 minutes.

Transfer the rice to a large bowl and allow the mixture to cool to lukewarm. Stir in the raisins with the liqueur, lemon zest, orange peel, almonds, eggs, salt, and cinnamon. Slowly stir in the heavy cream and mix well.

Transfer the mixture to the prepared pan. Place the pan in a larger pan and carefully pour hot water into the large pan to a depth of 1 inch.

Bake the cake until a skewer inserted in the center comes out clean but not dry, about 45 minutes.

Remove the cake pan from the water bath and cool it on a rack. Use a butter knife to loosen the cake around the edges of the pan and carefully invert the cake onto a serving dish. Remove and discard the parchment paper.

Serve the cake cut into wedges with a dollop of mascarpone cheese or whipped cream. Garnish with an orange segment or strawberry.

The cake can also be made in a buttered and floured 9 × 2-inch ring pan.

In the Shadow of the Medici

Piselli alla Fiorentina
(Peas Florentine Style)

Spinaci alla Fiorentina
(Spinach with Cream Sauce)

Zucchine Ripiene allo Zenzero
(Stuffed Zucchini with Ginger)

Mele con la Salsa di Lampone
(Apples with Raspberry Sauce)

YOU CANNOT GO to Florence—or to any other part of Tuscany, for that matter—and not hear the name Medici in many contexts, including the Medici Palace, Gardens, and any number of other structures bearing the Medici name. This powerful ruling family shaped the political and cultural nature of Tuscany from 1434 to 1743 and saw their greatest power flourish during the Renaissance in Florence. The Medici family produced bankers, popes, military leaders, and government officials, among others, and were responsible for commissioning some of the greatest works of Renaissance art.

Look on most Renaissance buildings in Tuscany and you are sure to see the Medici coat of arms, originally red balls against a gold shield. Over time the number of balls has changed from the original twelve to five. Some say the balls *(palle)* recall the family's origins as doctors *(medici)* or apothecaries. Others argue that they are coins inspired by the Guild of the Moneychangers, since the Medici were also bankers and merchants.

I would like to think that this privileged family also ate well, and I know from researching Italian cooking manuscripts that sumptuous meals were common in their day. And when they entertained it was for days, not a few hours, and could include up to dozens of opulent courses. One account I read mentions live birds flying out of pastry dough! All of this was meant to impress upon important guests the power of a ruling family.

The influence of the Medici is everywhere, even at the Mercato Centrale (central market) not far from Piazza di San Lorenzo near the family tombs.

Shoppers make their choices in the Mercato Centrale *in Florence.*

After visiting the tombs, I was famished and headed straight to the market to meet friends and our television crew. We wanted to capture on film what the market was all about, and why visitors from all over the world flock there. The market was built in 1874, a huge iron structure as large as a football field. Its two stories are to my way of thinking the "Internet" of *supermercati* (supermarkets) housing every imaginable type of food you could possibly crave. If you wanted a self-contained, guided tour of what constitutes Italian food, this would be the place to go. The best day to be there is Saturday when you can feel the kinetic energy of the throngs of shoppers.

I have been to this market many times, but on this particular visit I was experiencing it with my good friends Luciano and Anna Berti, who live in the city. Luciano shocked me with his matter-of-fact statement that this market is for tourists and not for the locals! We strolled through the first floor with its endless number of stalls selling meats and cheeses. Need a chicken? A rabbit? You'll purchase the whole animal, not cut-up pieces in Styrofoam containers. If you are really serious about Tuscan cooking, you will buy *trippa,* tripe, a Tuscan specialty that is the stomach lining of the cow, usually to be cooked with tomatoes and marjoram. Another specialty is *bistecca*, thick T-bone steak (p. 40) always served *al sangue* (rare). You can find *carne di cavallo* (horse meat), as well as *cinghiale,* (wild boar), another local favorite. Cured meats are plentiful, too, from the spicy Tuscan *finocchiona,* a dried sausage with lots of fennel seeds, to the mild-tasting classic prosciutto.

Just about any cheese that is made in Italy can be found there, from fresh *mozzarella di bufala* (buffalo mozzarella) to *taleggio,* a creamy cheese from Lombardia in the north, to cheeses I had never heard of. Of course, this being Tuscany, pecorino cheese is the favorite, especially the one produced in Pienza. And there are fresh pastas, the kind that are no longer made at home, including *pappardelle* (p. 22), wide noodles usually served with hare sauce, *pinci* (p. 119), a thick spaghetti often teamed with ragu sauce, and tagliatelle, ribbon-shaped noodles, also served with meat ragu. Just browsing there, it was hard to resist the temptation not to buy anything, but I really wanted those emerald green Tuscan olive oils, so I purchased several bottles, knowing that I would be hand-carrying them home.

On the second floor, Luciano led me down aisle after aisle of fresh and dried fruits. We sampled dried and sugared cherry tomatoes; they could pass for candy, but are better for you. Vibrant vegetables, spices, candies, flowers, herbs, and even packaged biscotti were all crowded into a space that was a memorable feast for the eyes. I saw the *zucca fiorentina* (Florentine squash) piled high in one stall, the very ones I grow in the *Ciao Italia* garden. A burst of deep violet color caught my attention in another stall . . . fabulous-looking *radicchio di Treviso* (elongated chickory from Treviso) used in salads, also popular grilled with a little olive oil. The artichokes from Puglia and Sicily made the most dramatic statement for me. They were displayed from large to small in various hues of green and violet and looked like a giant fan. Next to them were clusters of small, juicy red *pomodorini* that were each so large that I wondered why they are called small tomatoes. There was one stall that resembled a forest floor of mushrooms—sturdy porcini, a venerable favorite throughout Italy, chanterelles, and my favorite, *ovoli,* large mushrooms with an orange-yellow cap that were a favorite with Roman emperors and are often referred to as Caesar's mushrooms. These are rare outside of Italy. Luciano made sure I saw the *cavolo nero,* black cabbage similar to kale, an ancient vegetable depicted in paintings of market scenes of the Renaissance and popular in Tuscany to make a peasant soup called *ribolitta* (p. 210). Even the Medici considered it a favorite dish.

I knew what I wanted, *pesca bianca!* White peaches. These are addicting, with a perfume scent, smooth greenish skin, and buttery texture—but of course they were not in season yet, so I consoled myself with another piece of sugared *pomodoro.*

I chuckled when I spotted a sign that read "trip to hell," referring to *peperoncini,* dried red pepper flakes that wake up so many Italian dishes. I bought a bag to take home, along with the most colossal-looking capers packed in salt, from the island of Pantelleria. No Sicilian kitchen, least of all mine, should be without them, I told myself as my shopping bag ripped at the seam and I wondered if I had to buy another suitcase to get all the food home!

Plump packages of *arborio* rice for making risotto—already flavored with dried mushrooms, dried tomatoes, artichokes, peas, and lots of other ingredients—intrigued me. Seeing those prepackaged mixes made me wish that this kind of progress was not so forthcoming in Italy; but since convenience rules in the kitchen, even the market must cater to change.

The market tour worked up my appetite. I bought some fruit, cheese, and crusty bread as a *spuntino* (snack) for all of us as we headed outside. Near the market in the shadow of the Medici tombs, we found a place to sit down, enjoy our snack, and watch shoppers happily carry away edible treasures from *il Mercato Centrale*.

Piselli alla Fiorentina
Peas Florentine Style

SERVES 4

Peas are one of the first delights in my garden, and I like them small and almost raw in my cooking. In Tuscany they are prepared with a finely diced prosciutto.

Put the peas in a pot with the olive oil, garlic, parsley, and salt. Add just enough water to barely cover the peas and cook over medium-low heat, uncovered, for no longer than 2 minutes.

Gently stir in the prosciutto and sugar and cook 1 minute longer.

Serve the peas with some of the cooking liquid.

4 cups shelled fresh peas (about 2½ pounds)

¼ cup extra-virgin olive oil

1 teaspoon minced garlic

¼ cup diced parsley

¼ teaspoon fine sea salt

4 ounces diced prosciutto

1 teaspoon sugar

Spinaci alla Fiorentina
Spinach with Cream Sauce

SERVES 4

BESCIAMELLA SAUCE
MAKES 2 CUPS

2 tablespoons
unsalted butter

2 tablespoons unbleached
all-purpose flour

2 cups hot whole milk

Fine sea salt to taste

Coarse black pepper
to taste

FOR THE *SPINACI*

2 ten-ounce packages
fresh spinach, washed
and stemmed

2 tablespoons extra-virgin
olive oil

2 cloves garlic, minced

¼ teaspoon fine sea salt

¼ cup grated pecorino
cheese

*A*nything alla fiorentina, *meaning Florentine style, can often signify that there is spinach in the dish. In this preparation a white sauce* (besciamella) *provides added richness.*

Melt the butter in a saucepan over medium heat. Whisk in the flour to make a smooth paste. Slowly whisk in the milk and cook the mixture over medium heat until it thickens on the back of a spoon. Off the heat, stir in the salt and pepper. Cover and set aside.

Cook the spinach in a large pot without any additional water. When it is wilted, drain it and squeeze it dry.

Heat the olive oil in a sauté pan, add the garlic and the spinach, and cook, stirring with a wooden spoon for 3 or 4 minutes. Off the heat, stir in ½ cup of the *besciamella* sauce and transfer the mixture to a 9-inch Pyrex baking dish.

Spoon the remaining sauce over the top of the spinach and sprinkle with the cheese.

Bake about 15 minutes, or until the mixture is hot and the cheese has browned. Serve immediately.

Zucchine Ripiene allo Zenzero
Stuffed Zucchini with Ginger

SERVES 4

During the Renaissance it was a common practice to use lots of spices in food preparation, and it was a sign of wealth, since spices were so expensive. Ginger was used in many dishes and it is a nice addition to stuffed zucchini. Serve this for a light supper or luncheon with a side dish of roasted potatoes.

Cut each zucchini in half lengthwise and with a spoon scoop out the pulp, leaving a ¼-inch-thick walled shell. Drain the hollowed-out shells cut side down on paper towels.

Mash the pulp in a bowl with a fork, then mix in the ground round. Refrigerate the mixture.

Preheat the oven to 350°F.

Heat 1 tablespoon of the olive oil in a sauté pan and stir in the ginger and garlic and cook until both are softened. Stir in the pine nuts and cook 2 minutes longer. Transfer the mixture to the bowl with the pulp and meat mixture. Stir in the salt and lemon juice. Evenly divide and pack the mixture into the zucchini shells.

Place them in a lightly oiled casserole dish. Drizzle the remaining olive oil over the top and sprinkle on the cheese. Cover with foil and bake for 45 minutes. Uncover the dish and continue baking an additional 10 minutes, or until the meat mixture is nicely browned. Serve hot.

2 zucchini (1¼ pounds) about 8 inches long, stems trimmed

½ pound beef, ground round

2 tablespoons extra-virgin olive oil

1¼ teaspoons finely grated fresh ginger

1 teaspoon finely minced garlic

2 tablespoons pine nuts

1 teaspoon fine sea salt

1 teaspoon fresh lemon juice

4 tablespoons grated pecorino cheese

Mele con la Salsa di Lampone
Apples with Raspberry Sauce

SERVES 8 TO 10

2 cups fresh raspberries

3 tablespoons raspberry jam

2 tablespoons sugar

¼ cup white dessert wine such as Moscato d'Asti

1 to 2 tablespoons raspberry vinegar

8 to 10 medium-size Golden Delicious apples, peeled, cored, and thinly sliced

Mascarpone cheese or sweetened whipped cream

½ cup crushed almonds

Going through the Mercato Centrale *in Florence and admiring the variety of fruits and vegetables conjured up all kinds of ideas that I was eager to try when I got home. The unbelievably plump raspberries grabbed my attention because they were as big as gum balls and were just begging me to make one of my standby, quick company desserts, apples with raspberry sauce.*

Puree the raspberries in a blender or food processor. Add the jam and sugar and pulse to blend. Add the wine and vinegar and blend well.

Put the apple slices in a large bowl and pour the raspberry sauce over them. Mix gently to coat the apple slices. Cover the bowl and refrigerate the mixture for 1 hour.

Spoon the fruit with some of the sauce into individual dessert bowls and top with a dollop of mascarpone cheese or whipped cream. Sprinkle the almonds over the top of each bowl and serve immediately.

NOTE: To keep raspberries fresh and prevent mold, remove them from their container and place in a single layer on a paper towel–lined dish. Cover and refrigerate.

Practicing Al Fresco

Al fresco literally means "in the open air." For Italians, this means to be able to enjoy their dining experiences outdoors most of the year, but it also means "to be seen." One of the true experiences of observing daily life as it unfolds in Italy is to watch people practicing the art of *al fresco*. It is akin to being in a dress rehearsal for a Fellini film. Much of the theatrics takes place at open-air restaurants around the central piazza, or at tables crouched together on side streets with traffic whizzing by so close that it is best to keep your feet tucked in beneath the table. *Al fresco* in Italy is all about body language.

This art form is especially popular in Florence near the Piazza Signoria, where many go to admire the Palazzo Vecchio. It is a crowded area, so when I spotted a table with an umbrella I grabbed it and sat down. My feet immediately thanked me. I was in no particular hurry that day, and a glance around told me that neither was anyone else. What I observed was the real meaning of *al fresco* for Italians . . . food, yes, but fashion and flirtation, too. At the table next to me there was a mysterious-looking gentleman in a perfectly tailored pin-striped suit, with gold cuff links that glistened in the sun. He was engrossed in a copy of the newspaper *Corriere della Sera* in one hand, a cigarette and Campari and soda in the other. Circles of cigarette smoke wafted my way and I wished that I had chosen another table, but *al fresco* also means putting up with annoyances. At another table I spotted a chic, miniskirted *bellezza* with long polished fingernails, dark glasses, and a Fendi scarf wrapped around a swanlike neck; she was twirling strands of fettucine daintily around her fork. Next to her a middle-age couple hardly noticing one another sipped their espresso and nibbled at their biscotti while pigeons circled at their feet waiting for any crumb that might luckily be theirs. And there were lovers dining *al fresco* as well, using all the body language they could muster to demonstrate their *emozione* on the worldwide stage of the piazza. There were also clergy in their somber Franciscan garb and sandals, walking among the diners and passing the alms plate, not taking no for an answer. Off in a corner there was a *zingara,* or gypsy, trying to relieve the weight of a young man's wallet while speaking kindly to him, and there was an itinerant flower seller convinced that each table needed to have a fresh rose or two.

Finally my waiter appeared. I ordered a *limoncello,* and before I could say, *"Mi porti un bicchiere d'aqua,"* he was gone, reappearing minutes later with a tall, frosty glass of really sour lemon liqueur. *Grazie.* I slipped on my sunglasses (it's more comfortable to be who you want to be behind them) and sipped my drink. But I was all wrong, I told myself as I tried to fit in by hiding my penny-loafered feet, a telltale label of *un'Americana,* under the table. What I needed were stiletto heels, more gold, a leather purse from Peruzzi, or at least a Gucci knockoff sold by hawkers on every street corner, and the latest cell phone to catch the minute-by-minute calls of someone who needs me at that very moment to talk about nothing. Ringing phones seem to invade everyone's private open space. But then I realized that the expressive nature of the Italians runs through everything that defines them as a culture, and there is no way that I can compete, even if Italian blood runs in my veins. They do life so well by living in the moment, which is *the* essential component to practicing the art of *al fresco.*

In Michelangelo's Neighborhood

*Gnocchi di Patate con Salsa
di Pecorino e Panna*
(Potato Gnocchi with Pecorino Cream Sauce)

Gnocchi di Spinaci e Ricotta
(Spinach and Ricotta Cheese Gnocchi)

Pecorino con Pepe Nero sott'Olio
(Pecorino Cheese with Black Peppercorns
in Olive Oil)

*Tagliatelle alle Scorzette
di Arancia e Limone*
(Ribbon Noodles with Orange and
Lemon Zest)

Pecorino e Fave
(Pecorino Cheese and Fava Beans)

SETTIGNANO IS AN UNASSUMING town of Roman origin that overlooks the *colle armonioso,* the harmonious hills of Florence, and until I visited there to shoot an episode of *Ciao Italia,* I had no idea that it was important for several reasons. It was where Michelangelo's father brought him after his birth on March 6, 1475, and entrusted him to the care of a wet nurse, the wife of a stonecutter, and where he would return time and again in his formative years. It is said that this is where he developed his love for working with stone. In fact, many other sculptors also lived in Settignano because of its proximity to the nearby caves and stone quarries. Many painters and architects lived there as well.

It is also home to Enoteca La Sosta del Rossellino, a small Michelin Guide–rated wine bar and restaurant named after famous sculptor Antonio Gamberelli del Rossellino, born there in 1427. An *enoteca* is a wine "library," a place to sample the wines of the regions of Italy, and the owners of La Sosta del Rossellino, Damiano Miniera and his daughter Silvia, strive to maintain the establishment's reputation for superior wine and food. Damiano is an animated, gregarious, good-natured chef who was born in Corleone, Sicily. He likes to be innovative with ingredients, combining classical dishes with his interpretations. Silvia is in charge of the wines and knows just the right ones to pair with her father's creations.

When I arrived Damiano explained that *sosta* means a place to rest, where meals are not hurried. That sounded good to me as I donned an apron to help him make the potato gnocchi that are so popular on the evening menu. The dish

Damiano Miniera's light-as-a-cloud potato gnocchi, all ready for me to sample.

surprised me, because in my experience in Tuscany, spinach and ricotta gnocchi are more common than potato gnocchi. But these are a staple on *his* menu, and his customers would be disappointed if they were not available.

The kitchen is small but functional, like most restaurant kitchens in Italy. Yellow potatoes cooling in a large pot were ready, and Damiano quickly peeled and riced them. A pinch of salt and we were ready to form the gnocchi. No flour? He pursed his lips, gave me a quick stare, and said, *"Senza farina."* No flour, unless the potatoes are too soft to hold together.

There are so many different ways to make potato gnocchi in my family that heated arguments develop as to whose method is the best. Should there be flour, and what kind—regular, or potato flour; should there be eggs, maybe only the white, or the yolk? Some will shrug emphatically at the thought of using eggs at all. Too leaden!

With deft hands, Damiano shaped long ropes of potatoes on a lightly floured board then cut them into half-inch, plump pillows. As he did this I couldn't help but think that making gnocchi is not so different from Michelangelo chiseling away at stone. Both the cook and the sculptor's hands know when the feel is right.

Damiano lowered spoonfuls of gnocchi into the boiling water. They bobbed to the top in less than a minute, and he fished them out with a skimmer and placed them on a plate.

The sauce was not the usual tomato-basil one expects with potato gnocchi. Instead, Damiano melted marzolino (a pecorino cheese made in March, from which its name derives) and heavy cream in a saucepan. He spooned the sauce over the top. They were delicate-looking in their white blanket and tasted luscious. No lead sinkers there!

Next it was Silvia's turn to talk about the wines of the *enoteca*. We moved into the dining room, its walls lined with shelves holding wines from Tuscany and all over Italy. We sampled Petra Val di Cornia, D'Ovidio, and my favorite, Brunello di Montalcino, as well as Supertuscans (blends of Sangiovese with, most commonly, small amounts of Cabernet Savignon or Merlot), Chianti, and others along with a variety of cheeses. (My favorite was goat cheese served with applesauce and mint, but the aged pecorino drizzled with honey was just as good.) Later Damiano complimented the wines with a sampling of the dinner menu; the tagliatelle with lemon and orange juices and heavy cream was especially spectacular. The *carpaccio di maiale* (thin slices of cured pork) with pistachio nuts was a dish made from sheer genius!

The hour is growing late, and the view from the *enoteca* overlooking the harmonious hills is one of twinkling lights for as far as can be seen. It is magical, made more so when you realize that Michelangelo walked these streets, lived here as a boy, and found the inspiration for his majestic works of art from the sleepy town of Settignano.

Gnocchi di Patate con Salsa di Pecorino e Panna
Potato Gnocchi with Pecorino Cream Sauce

SERVES 6 TO 8 AS A FIRST COURSE

SAUCE

1 cup young pecorino cheese, cut into small pieces

⅔ cup heavy cream

Coarse black pepper to taste

DOUGH

6 large Yukon Gold potatoes, scrubbed

1 to 1½ teaspoons fine sea salt

Semolina flour as needed

Potato starch as needed

*D*amiano loves to mix and match the traditional dishes of Italy, and his potato gnocchi with a pecorino cheese sauce is a perfect example. He uses only two ingredients, potatoes and a hint of flour, and his fingers tell him when the dough is just right. Creating the dough "off the cuff" can be a daunting proposition, especially when making gnocchi, which can turn out to be lead sinkers instead of fluffy dumplings. The best advice I can give is to go by feel, and use trial-and-error. Potato gnocchi are usually topped with a fresh tomato sauce, but here again Damiano shows his ingenuity by making a quick sauce from pecorino cheese and cream.

Put the cheese and cream in a small saucepan and heat it until the cheese melts. Mix the sauce so it is smooth; cover, set aside, and keep warm while making the gnocchi.

Put the potatoes in a large pot and cover them with cold water. Bring to a boil and cook potatoes until they are fork-tender. Drain and cool the potatoes, then peel them.

Rice the potatoes into a large bowl or mash them using a hand masher. Stir in the salt to taste.

Lightly spread a work surface with a thin layer of semolina flour. Divide the potato mixture into 4 sections and work with 1 at a time. Roll the potatoes under the palm of your hand on the floured surface to form a long rope about the thickness of your middle finger. Cut one small piece and drop it into a small pan of boiling water to see if it will hold together without breaking up in the water. If it holds together, cut the remaining rope into 1-inch pieces and place them in single layers on floured towels. If the dough does not hold together, remix all the potatoes with a little bit of potato starch, using 1 tablespoon at a time and testing as above until the gnocchi hold together.

Continue making gnocchi until all the dough is used.

Bring a large pot of water to a boil and add 1 tablespoon of salt. Gently lift the towels with the gnocchi and shake them into the boiling water. They will not take long to cook, only a minute, or until they bob to the top.

Remove them with a slotted strainer, making sure to shake off the excess water and place them on a platter.

Pour the warm sauce over the top and give the gnocchi a grinding of pepper. Serve at once.

Gnocchi di Spinaci e Ricotta
Spinach and Ricotta Cheese Gnocchi

SERVES 8 TO 10 (ABOUT FORTY 1½-INCH GNOCCHI)

2½ cups fresh whole-milk ricotta

2 pounds fresh spinach, washed and stemmed

⅔ cup grated Parmigiano-Reggiano cheese

2 extra-large eggs

12 mint leaves, minced

1 teaspoon sea salt

½ teaspoon grated nutmeg

Dash white pepper

1¾ cup (approximately) unbleached all-purpose flour

12 tablespoons unsalted butter

10 small sage leaves, minced

Spinach and ricotta gnocchi are a first course reserved for my very favorite guests, and they are a traditional Tuscan favorite. These have a vibrant, forest green color and are light and fluffy. As with most dough preparations for gnocchi, it is the amount of flour used that will determine whether the texture is light or leaden. Be sure to squeeze as much water as possible out of the spinach or you will end up using too much flour. Patience is a virtue when making gnocchi.

Drain the ricotta cheese in a cheesecloth-lined strainer set over a bowl until it is very dry. Transfer the cheese to a large bowl and set aside.

Cook the spinach in batches in a covered large soup pot with no additional water until it has wilted. Drain in a colander, and when cool enough to handle squeeze the spinach as dry as possible with your hands to remove excess water. You should have about 2 cups of squeezed spinach.

Chop the spinach coarsely then puree it in a blender or food processor until it is very smooth. Transfer the spinach to the bowl with the cheese and stir in ⅓ cup of the grated cheese, eggs, mint, salt, nutmeg, and pepper and mix well. Begin adding the flour a little at a time until a soft dough is obtained and it is not sticking to your hands. (It is easier to form the gnocchi if the dough is refrigerated for several hours or overnight.)

Lightly flour a work surface. Using two soupspoons, shape heaping tablespoons of the dough into an oval or egg shape, then gently slide the dough off the spoon onto the floured surface.

Bring a large pot of salted water to a boil. With a slotted spoon, scoop up about 8 or 10 gnocchi at a time and add them to the water. Boil them until they float.

Meanwhile, melt the butter in a large sauté pan and stir in the sage leaves. Cover the pan and keep the sauce warm.

Use a slotted spoon to remove and transfer the gnocchi to the sauce, tossing them gently until well-coated with the sauce.

Divide between 8 individual plates and sprinkle with the remaining ½ cup of cheese. Serve hot.

Pecorino con Pepe Nero sott'Olio
Pecorino Cheese with Black Peppercorns in Olive Oil

1 pound aged pecorino cheese with black or green peppercorns

Dried red pepper flakes

Extra-virgin olive oil

Silvia knows her cheeses as well as her wines, and in Tuscany it is all about pecorino Toscano, sheep's milk cheese made between September and June. Pecorino Toscano is a table and grating cheese. When young it is soft and mild-tasting, but as it ages it hardens and develops a drier texture and a more pronounced taste. Pienza, a wonderful Renaissance town near the wine area of Montalcino, and home to Pope Pius XI, was partially designed by Bernardo Rossellino and is known for its pecorino cheese, which was also a favorite of Michelangelo. Pecorino with peppercorns is also a favorite of mine, and I like to give it marinated in olive oil as a gift from my kitchen. Serve it with crusty Tuscan bread (p. 94) and drizzle some of the oil from the cheese jar over the bread. Add a few olives and you have a simple antipasto.

Cut the cheese into small cubes and put them into 8- or 12-ounce jars. Sprinkle a few red pepper flakes in the jar. Fill the jars with the oil, making sure to cover the cheese completely. Cap and refrigerate. To use, bring the jars to room temperature. Serve the cheese with some of the oil along with bread.

The cheese will keep for several weeks in the refrigerator. Be sure any remaining cheese is covered with oil before placing it back in the refrigerator.

Tagliatelle alle Scorzette di Arancia e Limone

Ribbon Noodles with Orange and Lemon Zest

SERVES 4

*D*amiano serves tangy tagliatelle in an orange, lemon, and cream sauce to many adoring customers who cannot get enough of this heavenly dish. It is light and delicate with a deep citrus flavor. The sauce makes two cups and is enough to dress a pound of tagliatelle, ¼-inch-wide ribbon noodles that are similar to fettucine.

Use a zester to remove the orange and lemon peels in long strips, being careful not to take any of the bitter pith (white part) under the skin. You will need ¼ cup of the orange zest and 2 tablespoons of the lemon zest. Place the zests in a small saucepan. Cover them with water and boil for 5 minutes to remove any bitterness, then drain and refresh them under cold water. Pat them dry and set aside.

Cut the oranges and lemons in half and juice them. You will need ½ cup of orange and ¼ cup of lemon juice. Set the juices aside.

Melt the butter over medium heat in a 1-quart saucepan. Cook the shallots in the butter until they are very soft, but do not let them brown. Pour in the wine, raise the heat to high and cook 1 minute. Lower the heat and slowly stir in the cream. Slowly bring the mixture back to a boil and cook 2 minutes. Lower the heat to medium, stir in the orange and lemon zests and the orange and lemon juices. Let the sauce reduce over low heat to ⅓ its original volume. Season with salt and pepper and keep the sauce covered and warm while the tagliatelle are cooking.

Cook the tagliatelle according to the directions on p. 23. Drain and place them in a shallow bowl or platter. Pour the sauce over the top of the tagliatelle and toss to mix well. Stir in the parsley, correct the salt if necessary, and serve immediately.

2 medium-size oranges

2 medium-size lemons

2 tablespoons unsalted butter

2 tablespoons minced scallions or shallots

⅓ cup dry white wine

1½ cups heavy whipping cream

Fine sea salt to taste

Coarse white pepper to taste

2 tablespoons finely diced parsley

1 pound homemade or store-bought tagliatelle or fettucine

Legend has it that a Bolognese cook first made long ribbons of noodles called tagliatelle from the word tagliare ("to cut") after being inspired by the long blond hair of Lucrezia Borgia when she arrived in 1487 to marry the Duke of Este.

Pecorino e Fave
Pecorino Cheese and Fava Beans

SERVES 6 TO 8 AS AN ANTIPASTO

1 pound aged pecorino
cheese at room
temperature

3 pounds shelled fava
beans

Fine sea salt

*O*ne of the ways Tuscans enjoy pecorino cheese is as an antipasto
with fresh, shelled fava beans and a glass of wine. When the
beans are young and tender they need no cooking and can be eaten
raw. If they are large, boil them until the outer skin easily slips off.

Put the cheese on a cheese board and the fava beans in a bowl.
Have a small bowl of salt. Cut off bite-size pieces of cheese with a
cheese knife and eat it with the fava beans, dipping them first in
salt if you wish.

Sauce Sense

Pappardelle con la Salsa di Funghi Misti
(Wide Noodles with Mixed Mushroom Sauce)

Penne ai Pomodori Crudi
(Penne with Uncooked Tomato-Olive Sauce)

Penne con la Salsa di Ricotta
(Penne with Ricotta Cheese Sauce)

Salsa di Noci (Walnut Sauce)

Salsa Fresca di Pomodoro
(Fresh Tomato Sauce)

Salsa di Pinoli (Pine Nut Sauce)

SAUCE, *salsa* in Italian, is derived from the Latin *saltus,* or salted. History records that some of the first so-called sauces to come out of Italy were not very palatable. One of the first was fish, or *garum,* sauce recorded in the culinary writings of Apicius, a Roman gourmand from the first century A.D. In his time sauces were more like juices (from *ius*) and were thickened with bread. *Garum* was a concoction of pulverized fish, such as anchovy, wine, and bread mixed together. According to Harold McGee's book *On Food and Cooking*, primitive sauces like *garum* were used more to mask a flavor than to enhance it.

The French are legendary for their wonderful sauces, and indeed, if you are training as a chef, you had better know how to perfect such standard sauces as béchamel, mayonnaise, hollandaise, and *veloute*. By contrast, the Italian kitchen has no standardized sauces, and it would be difficult to give a concise list, owing to the fact that each region of Italy has its unique way of making them. Home cooks and professional chefs prefer making sauces from fresh vegetables and herbs, as in pesto sauce, the signature sauce of the region of Liguria—and, of course, tomato sauce put the region of Campania, and all of southern Italy, on the map in the nineteenth century; since then, tomato-based sauces are present in dishes from the top to the toe of the boot. *Besciamella,* a white cream sauce made with milk, butter, flour, and salt, is said to have come to Italy from France. But simply sautéing some onions in olive oil can make a wonderful sauce, or crushing up a garlic clove and warming it in olive oil.

A sauce in the hands of an Italian cook becomes an original creation. I like to make sauces straight from the garden, whether smooth in texture like pesto, parsley, and tomato sauces, or with more texture like zucchini, onion, or olive sauces.

Be sparing with your sauces. They are meant to be condiments, to add flavor and compliment the food that you are preparing—and the best part is that they take only minutes to prepare.

THICK OR THIN

Some cooks prefer thin sauces. Here is my rule of thumb as to how much flour is necessary to achieve thin to thicker sauces.

THIN: 1 tablespoon of flour for 1 cup of liquid

MEDIUM: 2 tablespoons of flour for 1 cup of liquid

THICK: 3 tablespoons of flour for 1 cup of liquid

Pappardelle con la Salsa di Funghi Misti
Wide Noodles with Mixed Mushroom Sauce

SERVES 4 TO 6

Wild mint is the distinguishing flavor in this mushroom sauce for pappardelle, *the wide noodle so popular in Tuscany. Teamed with an orchestra of assorted mushrooms—porcini, porto-bello, shitake, and oyster—it is easy to make and elegant enough for company. Traditionally this dish is served* senza formaggio *(without cheese).*

Heat 1 tablespoon of the olive oil in a sauté pan and cook the garlic until it is soft but not browned. Add the mushrooms along with the remaining olive oil and cook until they soften and render their juices. Stir in the tomatoes, salt, and pepper and cook the sauce covered, over low heat for 2 to 3 minutes. Stir in the mint and cook 1 minute longer. Turn off the heat and keep the sauce covered while the *pappardelle* cook.

Cook the *pappardelle* according to the directions on p. 23. Reserve ¼ cup of cooking water and add it to the sauce. Transfer the *pappardelle* to a bowl, stir in the sauce, and serve piping hot.

NOTE: Adding herbs when a dish is almost cooked preserves more of their essential oils than adding them at the beginning; too much cooking will destroy their flavor.

⅓ cup extra-virgin olive oil

3 cloves garlic, minced

12 ounces assorted mushrooms (portobello, oyster, shitake, etc.), stemmed and thinly sliced

3 pounds fresh tomatoes, skinned, seeded, and chopped

Salt and pepper to taste

½ cup fresh mint, minced

½ pound store-bought or homemade *pappardelle* (p. 22)

Penne ai Pomodori Crudi
Penne with Uncooked Tomato-Olive Sauce

SERVES 4 TO 6

2 pounds plum tomatoes, peeled, seeded, and cut into small pieces

1 cup mixed pitted olives in oil, drained and cut into small pieces

2 tablespoons capers in salt, rinsed and diced

1 large clove garlic, minced

⅓ cup parsley, minced

6 or 7 large basil leaves, torn into small pieces

½ cup extra-virgin olive oil

Fine sea salt to taste

Course black pepper to taste

1 pound penne

This summertime, no-cook tomato sauce is perfect for penne served at room temperature.

Early in the day combine the tomatoes, olives, capers, garlic, parsley, basil, olive oil, salt, and pepper in a large bowl. Cover and set aside to marinate at room temperature.

Cook the penne al dente, as described on p. 23, drain it, and toss it with the tomato mixture. Serve at room temperature.

For variety, add chopped red and yellow bell peppers and cooked, diced artichoke hearts.

Penne con la Salsa di Ricotta
Penne with Ricotta Cheese Sauce

SERVES 4 TO 6

A container of rich-tasting ricotta cheese is always on the shelf in my refrigerator. I use it to stuff vegetables, to mix into fluffy frittatas, of course to stuff pasta, and to make cheesecake—and I like it as a sauce for penne, the slant-cut pasta that is a favorite in Tuscany. This effortless sauce is ready in minutes because it is uncooked.

Spread the ricotta in a thin layer in a casserole dish large enough to hold the cooked penne. Sprinkle the pecorino and Parmigiano-Reggiano cheeses over the ricotta. Sprinkle the butter over the cheese and then grind the pepper over the butter. I set the dish on top of the pasta pot to keep it warm and melt the butter while bringing the pasta water to a boil.

Cook the penne until it is al dente in 4 to 6 quarts of rapidly boiling water to which 1 tablespoon of salt has been added. Drain the penne and add it with two tablespoons of the cooking water to the ricotta-lined casserole dish. Mix quickly to make a creamy consistency with the ricotta. Add salt to taste. Serve at once with lots of coarse black pepper.

1½ cups ricotta cheese, well-drained

⅔ cup grated pecorino cheese

½ cup grated Parmigiano-Reggiano cheese

6 tablespoons unsalted butter, cut into bits

Coarse black pepper to taste

Fine sea salt to taste

1 pound penne

2 tablespoons reserved cooking water

Salsa di Noci
Walnut Sauce

MAKES 1 CUP, ENOUGH FOR
4 FIRST-COURSE SERVINGS

3 cloves garlic, peeled

1 medium shallot, peeled

1 cup walnut halves

10 to 12 fresh sage
leaves, stems removed

½ cup extra-virgin
olive oil

½ teaspoon fine sea salt

2 tablespoons reserved
cooking water

8 ounces spaghetti,
fettucine, or penne

*I took my inspiration for this walnut sauce from the Renaissance,
when nuts were used in sauces for meats and fowl. The nuts were
pulverized in a mortar and pestle until reduced to a fine bread-crumb
texture, then combined with spices and broth to be transformed into
sauce. There are many variations on walnut sauce; in this one I use
some of the classic elements found in the Tuscan kitchen: good olive
oil; fresh sage leaves, and garlic.*

On a cutting board, mince the garlic and shallots together.

Mince the walnuts and sage leaves together and set aside.

Heat the olive oil in a large sauté pan, add the garlic and shallots, and cook them over medium heat until the garlic softens but
does not brown. Stir in the walnut mixture and cook for two or
three minutes. Stir in the salt. Cover the pan and keep the sauce
warm while the pasta cooks.

Cook the pasta in 4 quarts of rapidly boiling water with 1
tablespoon of salt until it is al dente. Drain the pasta, reserving 2
tablespoons of the cooking water.

Stir the pasta and reserved water into the nut sauce and reheat
everything quickly over medium heat until the pasta is well-coated.
Transfer the pasta to a serving dish.

If you wish, pass grated pecorino cheese to sprinkle on top.

Salsa Fresca di Pomodoro
Fresh Tomato Sauce

MAKES ABOUT 3¼ CUPS

There is nothing like the taste of garden-ripe tomatoes—for salads and for making this wonderful fresh tomato sauce. I like to use plum tomatoes, which are meaty, not watery. In this preparation all the ingredients are slowly cooked together for an hour until everything is very soft and a lot of the liquid has evaporated. Then everything is transferred to a food processor and zip, zip—a beautiful, smooth sauce is created that is just right on pasta and fish. Make a few batches for the freezer. Use half the sauce recipe for ½ pound of cooked spaghetti.

Fill a large pot with water and bring it to a boil. Add the tomatoes and blanch them until the skins start to separate. Remove the tomatoes with a slotted spoon to a bowl. When cool enough to handle, peel and discard the skins. Coarsely chop the tomatoes and set aside.

Heat the olive oil in a saucepan, stir in the carrots, celery, and onion. Cook 1 minute. Stir in the tomatoes. Cover the pot, reduce the heat to simmer, and cook the ingredients for 1 hour, or until everything is very soft and the mixture has thickened.

Five minutes before the sauce is cooked stir in the basil and parsley.

Transfer the mixture to a food processor and puree until the sauce is smooth. Transfer the sauce to a saucepan, stir in the salt. The sauce is ready to use or freeze.

2¼ pounds plum tomatoes, cored

4 tablespoons extra-virgin olive oil

2 carrots, thinly sliced

1 rib celery, thinly sliced

1 medium onion, peeled and thinly sliced

8 large fresh basil leaves, torn into pieces

5 sprigs fresh parsley, leaves only

1½ to 2 teaspoons salt or to taste

Salsa di Pinoli
Pine Nut Sauce

½ cup bread crumbs

1½ tablespoons white vinegar

4 ounces pine nuts

2 anchovy filets in oil, drained

1 teaspoon sugar

Olive oil

Salt and pepper to taste

Juice of ½ lemon

This pine nut sauce is often served with boiled meats, but I also like it with fish. The preparation is traditionally made in a mortar with a pestle, but a food processor makes for quick work.

Moisten the bread crumbs with the vinegar in a small bowl. Transfer the bread crumbs to a food processor with the pine nuts, anchovies, and sugar. Pulse everything until it is smooth. Drizzle a little olive oil through the feed tube with the motor running to create a creamy consistency. Add salt and pepper and the lemon juice.

Signature Sweets of Siena

Panforte (Fruitcake)

Cavallucci (Little Horses)

Cenci (Powdered Sugar Strips)

Crescentine Salate (Salted Pizza Bites)

Pan di Ramerino
(Rosemary and Raisin Rolls)

Ricciarelli di Siena
(Siena-Style Almond Cookies)

IT IS A SHAME THAT so many visitors to Tuscany choose only to spend time in Florence, bypassing the equally exquisite-art-filled city of Siena in central Tuscany. It is a city with a past love-hate relationship with Florence since the Florentines were defeated by the Sienese at the battle of Montaperti in the thirteenth century, and to this day the Sienese have not let the Florentines forget it. Most people who visit identify the city with its most famous event, the *Palio,* a crazed, gladiatorial horse race that takes place every July and August, and the preparation for which consumes the energies of the population all year long. It is what the Sienese live for.

Besides the world-renowned *Palio,* Siena can boast its being the home of the first modern bank, started in the thirteenth century, home of Saint Catherine of Siena, the city's patron, who was influential in persuading Pope Gregory XI to return the seat of the Papacy to Rome after sixty-seven years of exile in Avignon, home to one of the most spectacular black-and-white-marble-striped cathedrals in the world, and home to *panforte,* the classic sweet bread with a history that goes back to the Middle Ages. The best place to get it is at Nannini, on Via Banchi di Sopra 24, the most famous pastry shop in the city. The Nannini family is one of the oldest in Siena and also has a reputation as fine makers of *cenci, cantucci,* and *ricciarelli,* the other signature sweets of Siena. I entered this sugary world early one day to film just how important these confections are to the Sienese. Step into Nannini's and you enter a world lit by glass chandeliers that look like large rosettes. Beautiful dark wooden shelves line the lemon yellow–painted walls that are stocked with beautifully packaged biscotti, *cantucci,* and *panforte.* Walk along

Nannini's in Siena, the pastry shop known worldwide for its panforte, ricciarelli, *and many other sweets and savories.*

the gleaming terra-cotta and white-colored marble floors and peer into gorgeous glass cases displaying exotic confections that can break the will of even the most die-hard dieter. Drool over miniature, golden custard tarts, fruit-glazed tarts, order *panini* to go with fillings of ham, mozzarella cheese, and tomato, or with vegetarian fillings. Wonder at the marzipan fruits that could pass for just being plucked from their stems, or puffy donuts with cream fillings peeking out around their edges, or slick, smooth, chocolate-glazed sacher torte; or delight in delicate meringues so fragile that they shatter upon one bite, slender *savoiardi* (ladyfingers), good all by themselves, or used in tiramisu, and of course classic *panforte,* sold whole or by the slice.

For the television segment I enlisted the help of Mirila, a petite, smartly dressed woman with a gracious smile and who has been working at Nannini's for longer than she cared to say, and who assured me that she knew her pastries.

I was mesmerized by the history lesson Mirila delivered about *panforte,* which loosely translated means "strong bread" though its real meaning is derived from the term *fortis,* meaning sour. During the Middle Ages a flat-breadlike focaccia was made from wheat flour and water and embellished with the addition of honey, and the bread was called *melatello.* When fruits were in season they were added to the dough. Unfortunately, the fruit remained moist in the bread after baking, and in warm weather the bread turned sour, probably from the fermentation of the fruits. So the new name, *panforte,* was born. Over the centuries, baking techniques were perfected by nuns in convent kitchens and *panforte* and other baked goods were sold to the public to raise necessary funds. This was helped along with the donation of expensive spices to the convents by pilgrims returning from the orient. In the late nineteenth century, when the king and queen of Italy, Margherita of Savoy and her husband Umberto, came to Siena for the *Palio,* a special *panforte bianco* was made in her honor. The ingredients were candied fruits, almonds, sugar, honey, and marzipan flavored with cinnamon, nutmeg, and vanilla. You can still buy it today at Nannini's. Or you can make it at home (p. 170).

The next sweet to catch my fancy at Nannini's was *ricciarelli* (p. 178). According to legend, the name *ricciarelli* was given to this confection after Ricciardetto della Gherardesca, a Sienese who, upon returning to his home near Volterra from the Crusades, recounted seeing "foreign biscuits curled like the Sultan's slippers," triangular in shape and made from a dough of almonds, sugar, candied fruits, and vanilla flavoring. As time went on, the cookie took on the appearance of a diamond or an oval. One thing is certain: They are beloved by the Sienese, as evidenced by the way they were flying out of Nannini's.

Mirila passed around a tray of *cantucci,* a sophisticated name for what we know as biscotti, hard biscuits great for dunking in wine or coffee. It seems the original *cantucci* came from the Medici court, whose bakers learned how to make them from the confectioners who came to Tuscany in the service of Elizabeth d'Este in the fifteenth century. *Cantucci,* also called *morselletti* (little bites), are made with sugar, eggs, almonds, and vanilla flavoring, although I suspect some of them also were flavored with jasmine water. The traditional way to eat them is to dunk them in a glass of Tuscan Vin Santo, a dessert wine. Mirila offers these as well, explaining that, depending on where one travels in Tuscany, this cookie is known by various names and ingredients. We all agree that *panforte, ricciarelli,* and *cantucci* are worth the trip to Siena, a city that knows how to achieve sweet success.

Panforte
Fruitcake

SERVES 8–10

⅔ cup hazelnuts

½ cup slivered almonds

½ cup diced candied
orange peel

½ cup diced candied
lemon peel

¼ cup Dutch-process
cocoa, such as Droste

½ cup unbleached all-
purpose flour

1 teaspoon ground
cinnamon

½ teaspoon ground
nutmeg

½ teaspoon ground cloves

¼ teaspoon mace

¼ teaspoon coriander

¼ teaspoon white or
black pepper

½ cup sugar

½ cup honey

1 drop cinnamon oil or
1 teaspoon of vanilla

Rice paper (optional)

Confectioner's sugar

Panforte *is probably the most revered cake at Nannini's in Siena. You can tell by just looking at it that it is a chewy, dense fruitcake chock-full of spices, fruit, and nuts. Because of all the spices, panforte had a long shelf life and was even carried into battle as sustenance for hungry soldiers. Traditionally, edible rice paper lines the baking pan, but it is not critical. Wrapped in beautiful Florentine papers, often with historic scenes on them, this bread/cake makes a wonderful gift.*

Preheat the oven to 350°F.

Butter an 8-inch cake pan, line it with rice paper, cut to fit, or parchment paper. Butter the rice paper or parchment paper and set the pan aside.

Spread the hazelnuts on a baking sheet and toast them for 5 minutes. Let cool. Lower the oven temperature to 325°F.

Chop the hazelnuts and almonds coarsely. Transfer them to a glass bowl and stir in the candied peels, cocoa, flour, and spices; mix well. Set aside.

Combine the sugar and honey in a small saucepan; bring the mixture to a boil and cook for 3 or 4 minutes, or until the mixture registers 248°F on a candy thermometer, or a small amount dropped into cold water forms a ball when squeezed. Stir in the cinnamon or vanilla. Add the mixture to the dry ingredients and work quickly to mix everything well. The mixture will be stiff and sticky and hard to mix. I use a soupspoon to help gather up the ingredients.

Scoop and spread the mixture into the prepared cake pan. The mixture should be no more than ¼- to ½-inch thick in the pan. Keep a bowl of water handy and wet your hands to help you pat the mixture into the pan.

Bake for 25 minutes or until firm to the touch. While still warm, run a butter knife along the inside edge of the pan, then invert the cake onto a cooling rack. If you used parchment paper on the bottom of the cake, remove it and discard it. Carefully turn the cake right side up.

If you used rice paper, do not remove it. Allow the cake to cool for 5 minutes then turn it right side up.

Allow the cake to cool completely, then dust it liberally with confectioner's sugar.

Serve cut into thin wedges.

NOTE: Cake-decorating supply stores often have beautiful wrapping papers with Florentine and renaissance designs that are perfect for wrapping *panforte* to give as a gift.

Cavallucci
Little Horses

MAKES 3 DOZEN

1 cup water

1 cup granulated sugar

¼ cup honey

¼ cup candied orange peel

¼ cup raisins, chopped

½ cup walnuts, coarsely chopped

¼ cup almonds, coarsely chopped

2½ teaspoons baking powder

½ teaspoon ground cinnamon

½ teaspoon ground cloves

1 teaspoon aniseeds, crushed

⅛ teaspoon white pepper

2½ cups flour

These cookies were originally imprinted with the image of a horse, and were named for the cavalluccio, *or pony. They were first made for stablehands, who handled horses, but with a dough that was very plain. There have been many versions of the dough over the years—some flavored with cloves, cinnamon, candied fruits, and nuts. According to tradition, everyone in Siena eats two cavallucci and one piece of panforte at Christmastime.*

Preheat the oven to 350°F.

Line two baking sheets with parchment paper and set aside.

Bring the water to a boil in a large pot. Stir in the sugar until dissolved. Remove from heat and quickly stir in all the remaining ingredients except the flour. Mix until well blended. Stir in the flour. Allow mixture to cool for 20 minutes. The dough will be very heavy and it is best to chill it for several hours for easier handling.

Transfer the dough to a lightly floured surface and cut it into quarters. Roll each piece into an 18-inch rope and cut 2-inch pieces with a knife. Make a thumb print in each piece and place them ½ inch apart on the baking sheets. Bake for 18 to 20 minutes, or until the cookies are lightly browned on the bottom. They will be hard when removed from the oven but will soften as they cool.

Cenci
Powdered Sugar Strips

MAKES 6½ TO 7 DOZEN

One of the most familiar treats in Nannini's pastry-shop display cases are mounds of crispy, sugared strips called cenci, *which we made at home and called "rags," but* cenci *sounds more elegant. These randomly cut pieces of orange- or lemon-scented dough are fried and then coated in confectioner's sugar. In Tuscany at* Carnivale *time, this sweet treat is made everywhere, and everyone has their fill before the austere Lenten season begins. A pasta machine is perfect for thinning the dough.*

In a bowl, whisk together the sugar, butter, eggs, rum, zest, and salt. Stir in the flour and then use your hands to create a smooth ball of dough, or make the dough in a food processor. Put the dough in a bowl, cover it with plastic wrap and allow it to rest for an hour in the refrigerator.

Divide the dough into four pieces and work with one at a time.

To roll the dough out by hand, use a rolling pin and roll out each piece into a rectangle no more than ⅛ inch thick. Use a pastry wheel to cut irregular-shaped pieces about 5½ inches long and 2 inches wide. Make a 1-inch slit in the center of each piece, but do not cut to the ends. Place the pieces on clean towels until all the dough is used.

To thin the dough using a pasta machine, flatten the dough slightly with a rolling pin, then lightly dust it with flour and thin it in the machine using the roller section. I thin the dough to the highest number on my machine, which is 7, because I like my *cenci* thin; but adjust for thickness as you prefer.

Heat 6 cups of canola oil to 375°F in a deep fryer or in a heavy clad pot (test the temperature of the oil with a candy thermometer

¼ cup sugar

2 tablespoons unsalted butter, melted and cooled

2 large eggs

2 tablespoons rum, orange liqueur, or brandy

Grated zest of 2 large oranges or lemons

½ teaspoon salt

2 cups unbleached all-purpose flour

6 cups canola oil for frying

⅓ cup confectioner's sugar

if using a heavily clad pot). Fry the *cenci* a few at a time until golden brown. Drain them on paper towels.

While still warm, place the *cenci* in a clean paper bag with the confectioner's sugar. Close the top of the bag and shake gently to coat the *cenci*.

These are best served the day they are made. Try to eat just one!

Crescentine Salate
Salted Pizza Bites

MAKES AT LEAST 3½ DOZEN

Not everything at Nannini's is sweet; there are savory offerings, too, like vegetable-and-cheese minitarts, sandwiches with every type of meat and cheese or vegetable filling imaginable—and cres-centine, small pizzalike bread, studded with flecks of rosemary, that are deep-fried. They make a great snack or antipasto served with olives and slivers of pecorino cheese. The dough is easy to make in a food pro-cessor or by hand. Crescentine are best served warm the day they are made.

Mix the flour, salt, and baking powder together in a bowl. Work in the butter and rosemary, then add the wine a little at a time until a soft ball of dough is formed. Roll the dough into a 12 × 11-inch rectangle, then trim the piece to 10 × 10 inches. Cut 2-inch squares. Reroll the scraps to make more.

Heat the oil in a deep fryer or heavy-duty pot until a ther-mometer registers 375°F. Fry the *crescentine* in the oil until golden brown. Remove them with a slotted spoon to a baking sheet lined with paper towels. Sprinkle the *crescentine* with salt and serve warm.

VARIATION: Use a combination of herbs, or add ½ cup of minced prosciutto to the dough.

2 cups unbleached all-purpose flour

¾ teaspoon fine sea salt

2 teaspoons baking powder

2 tablespoons unsalted butter at room temperature

1½ tablespoons fresh rosemary needles, minced

⅔ cup dry white wine

4 cups vegetable oil

Coarse sea salt for sprinkling on top

Pan di Ramerino
Rosemary and Raisin Rolls

MAKES 1 DOZEN

DOUGH

1 package active dry yeast

1¾ cups warm water
(110°F)

1 tablespoon extra-virgin
olive oil

4 to 4½ cups unbleached
all-purpose flour

2 teaspoons fine sea salt

FILLING

3 tablespoons extra-virgin
olive oil

3 tablespoons fresh
rosemary needles, minced

½ cup chopped dark
raisins or ⅓ cup
whole currants

1 large egg, slightly
beaten

Nannini's is a favorite stop for hungry school children, who love to eat these delicious small rolls as a merenda (snack). At one time, women used to have these ready when children arrived home, but today they are usually store-bought.

Dissolve the yeast in ½ cup of the water in a large bowl. Stir to mix well and allow the yeast to get chalky-looking and bubbly, about 5 minutes. Stir in the remaining water and the olive oil.

Begin adding the flour one cup at a time to the yeast mixture, working it in with your hands until you have a rough-looking, shaggy mass of dough. Add the salt with the last addition of flour.

Turn the dough out onto a lightly floured surface and knead it with your hands until a soft ball of dough comes together that is not sticking to your hands. If you need more flour, add about 2 tablespoons at a time, otherwise a tough dough will result.

Lightly oil a large bowl with olive oil, add the dough, turning it in the bowl to coat it with the oil. Cover the bowl tightly with plastic wrap and allow it to double in size in a warm but not hot place.

Meanwhile, heat the olive oil in a small skillet over low heat. Stir in the rosemary needles and cook them for 2 minutes, pressing on them with the back of a wooden spoon to release their oil. Stir in the raisins or currants and cook for 1 minute.

Transfer the mixture to a bowl to cool.

Lightly grease two baking sheets with olive oil and set aside.

Punch down the dough and turn it out onto a lightly floured surface. Knead for 3 or 4 minutes until smooth and not sticky. Roll the dough into a 14-inch round and spread the rosemary mixture over it. Roll the dough up like a jelly roll, tucking in the ends as you go. Pinch the underside seam closed.

Fold the dough in half and knead it into a ball to distribute the filling. The dough will feel wet and sticky at first, but as you knead it, it will come together. Roll the dough out under the palms of your hands to form a long rope and cut it into 12 equal pieces.

Roll each piece into a smooth, round ball. Place the balls 1 inch apart on the baking sheets. Brush the tops with the beaten egg. Cover the balls with a clean towel and allow them to rise for 35 to 40 minutes, or until they are puffy-looking.

Preheat the oven to 375°F.

Just before baking, make an "x" in the top of each roll with a blade. Bake for 20 to 25 minutes, or until the rolls are nicely browned on top and bottom. Remove them to cooling racks and let cool completely.

NOTE: These freeze well if wrapped individually in aluminum foil and placed in Ziploc bags. Allow the rolls to defrost unwrapped at room temperature. Reheat them in a preheated 325°F oven for about 5 minutes.

Ricciarelli di Siena
Siena-Style Almond Cookies

MAKES ABOUT 4 DOZEN 3-INCH COOKIES

2½ cups slivered almonds

8 teaspoons powdered egg whites (see note)

½ cup warm water

2 cups granulated sugar

Grated zest of one large orange

Rice paper (optional)

Ricciarelli *(curls) are light-as-a-cloud almond meringue cookies that are also synonymous with Siena. In this adaptation I use powdered egg whites instead of fresh. This makes it unnecessary to waste egg yolks. Edible rice paper, which is part of the traditional method of making this cookie, is available at cake supply stores, but the cookies can be made without them.*

Line two baking sheets with parchment paper and set aside.

Preheat the oven to 325°F.

Grind the almonds in a food processor until reduced to a semi-fine powder. Leave some texture to the almonds. You should have about 2⅔ cups.

Whisk the powdered egg whites with the water in a small bowl. When completely blended, transfer the mixture to a stand mixer fitted with a wire whisk. Beat the egg-white mixture on high speed while adding the sugar a little at a time. Beat until the whites thicken, are shiny, and will not fall off a spoon when scooped from the bowl.

With a rubber spatula fold in the nuts and orange zest.

Fill a large, tipless pastry bag with some of the mixture and pipe 3-inch ovals, or diamond shapes, onto the parchment paper, spacing them 1 inch apart. Or use two spoons to scoop the mixture onto the parchment paper.

To bake the meringues using rice paper, lay the rice paper sheets over the parchment paper; you may have to use several sheets to make a single layer, depending on how wide and long the paper is. Then pipe the mixture over the rice paper leaving about 1 inch between each one.

Dust the tops of the cookies with confectioner's sugar.

Bake about 20 minutes, or until the *ricciarelli* are glossy-looking and firm to the touch, but pale-looking, not brown. They should have soft interiors.

Do not attempt to remove them immediately from the bake sheets—they will break. Allow them to cool about 15 minutes before transferring them to wire racks to cool completely.

If the *ricciarelli* were baked with rice paper, use a scissors to trim the edges of the rice paper to make them even with the cookies.

When completely cool redust the tops with confectioners' sugar.

NOTE: 2 teaspoons of powdered egg whites is equal to 1 fresh egg white.

A Chef Goes to Tuscany

Branzino alla Griglia
(Grilled Sea Bass)

Insalata di Melanzane e Fagiolini
(Grilled Eggplant and Green Bean Salad)

Insalata di Patate e Pomodorini
(Potato and Cherry-Tomato Salad)

Penne al Coccio
(Penne with Butter and Truffle Paste)

Zuccotto
(Pastry Cream and Fruit–Filled Sponge Cake)

CHEF RALPH CONTE began his culinary career at his Neapolitan grandmother's side, washing dishes and learning her home-cooking secrets. Years later her influence would be felt even more when he left home to live in Arezzo, Tuscany, for two years to learn the art of Tuscan cooking in the Hotel Drago's kitchen. While there, he managed to travel to all of the regions for a better understanding of Italian food.

Ralph has a unique sense of how to translate Tuscan food for an American clientele in his restaurant, Raphael Bar Bistro in Providence, Rhode Island. He is so passionate about what he serves that his pristine home garden is the source of most of the vegetables found on the restaurant's daily menu, including everything from weighty eggplants and porcelain-looking peppers, to Modigliani red tomatoes. He is also serious about his Italian wine cellar, which houses over four thousand bottles, 30 percent of which are Tuscan wines.

His home overlooking Narragansett Bay reflects his love for Italy, too, with its Tuscan villa–style architecture that blends perfectly with modern features: high ceilings, lots of glass, and a classic kitchen where Ralph spends much of his time creating recipes. Outside the kitchen door a beautiful flower-bedecked patio offers even more inspiration. Nearby, the best-looking herb garden I have ever seen provides all the flavor that is needed to complete the dishes that Ralph likes to cook on his outdoor grill.

When I spent the day with him filming a segment for *Ciao Italia*'s Tuscany series, I realized that Ralph's philosophy about cooking is a lot like mine: Use the freshest ingredients and keep the treatment simple. I call this minimalist cooking, meaning using less rather than more to bring out flavors, as was the case with the whole sea bass (p. 185) prepared on the grill that day and flavored with fresh rosemary, onions, and lemon juice. But don't just take my word for it—try Ralph's recipes in this chapter, and I think you will agree that his stay in Tuscany has served him well.

Branzino alla Griglia
Grilled Sea Bass

SERVES 4 TO 6

R alph Conte's Tuscan villa overlooking the ocean provides him with much inspiration. He is very serious about authentic cooking, as is evidenced by his beautiful wood-burning outdoor oven and grill where he bakes pizza and bread and grills succulent, whole sea bass. I was envious when he told me that he gets in his boat and fishes the waters for his catch, so I knew it just couldn't get any fresher than that. Sea bass has tough scales, so use a blunt knife or descaler to do the job and work from the tail toward the head. Sea bass is almost always sold whole, so if you are not going to catch it yourself, order it from a fishmonger.

Remove a 1-inch length of rosemary needles from the base of the sprigs. Soak 4 of the sprigs in a bowl of water for about 30 minutes so they are pliable; these will be used to close the cavity of the fish.

Combine the olive oil, the chili peppers, and the juice of one lemon in a small bowl. Stir in ¼ teaspoon of coarse salt and set aside.

To really cook the fish without it sticking to the grill, preheat the grill for about 15 minutes. While the grill is heating up, make ½-inch slits in the skin of the fish on both sides and insert the lemon slices.

Open the cavity of the fish and insert the onion rings, lemon wedges, and 1 teaspoon of coarse salt. Use the soaked rosemary sprigs to close the cavity by threading them through the skin opening from one side to the other.

Use the remaining sprig as a brush to baste the fish as it cooks.

Brush the fish with a little of the olive-oil mixture using the rosemary sprig; place the fish on the grill and baste occasionally. If

5 whole rosemary sprigs, about 8 inches long

½ cup extra-virgin olive oil

2 small red chili peppers, slit

1 small yellow chili pepper, slit

5 lemons, 2 cut into thin slices, 2 cut into wedges, and 1 juiced

Coarse sea salt

4½- to 5-pound whole, scaled, and gutted sea bass

2 onions, peeled and cut into thin rings

your grill is at 600°F the fish will cook in about 10 minutes. Turn it once halfway through the cooking, using a pair of wide, flat, metal spatulas.

Carefully remove the fish to a waiting platter when done; open the cavity and remove the rosemary sprigs and onions. With a small knife, peel back the skin of the fish and discard it. Cut the fish into pieces and serve with additional lemon wedges.

Insalata di Melanzane e Fagiolini
Grilled Eggplant and Green Bean Salad

SERVES 4 TO 6

*L*ike many Italian Americans who came to Rhode Island, Chef *Ralph Conte is doing a great job of keeping culinary traditions alive. His garden is his pride and solitude, and this eggplant-and-green-bean salad is just one example of his creativity in the kitchen. Make this early in the day for the best flavor. It is a great dish for* al fresco *dining.*

Preheat an outdoor grill.

Combine the garlic, lemon juice, ½ cup of the olive oil, salt, and pepper in a salad bowl. Set aside.

With a vegetable peeler, strip the eggplant skin lengthwise, and cut the eggplant into ½-inch-thick rounds.

Grill the slices, brushing them occasionally with the remaining olive oil. Ralph likes to do this with a rosemary sprig, but a brush will do. Do not let the slices get mushy; they should remain al dente.

Cut them into ½-inch strips and add them with the green beans to the bowl with the marinade. Toss gently. Add the mint leaves. Allow to sit at room temperature for several hours before serving. Accompany with Tuscan bread (p. 94)

2 cloves garlic, peeled and thinly sliced

Juice of 2 medium lemons

½ cup extra-virgin olive oil plus 2 tablespoons

¼ teaspoon fine sea salt

Coarse black pepper to taste

1 medium-size eggplant, stem top removed

2 cups cooked green beans, cut in half

½ cup whole mint leaves

Insalata di Patate e Pomodorini
Potato and Cherry-Tomato Salad

SERVES 4 TO 6

¾ cup extra-virgin
olive oil

6 tablespoons white wine
vinegar

1½ teaspoons fine sea salt

Coarse black pepper
to taste

2 pounds small white
potatoes, scrubbed

1½ cups cherry tomatoes,
cut in half

6 basil leaves torn into
small pieces

This simple potato and cherry-tomato salad is perfect for al fresco dining. Put it together early in the day and forget it. Ralph likes to use small white potatoes because of their creamy texture, and the salad is even more special when he adds sweet cherry tomatoes right from the garden.

Combine the olive oil, vinegar, salt, and pepper in a salad bowl and set aside.

Put the potatoes in a pot, cover them with cold water, and cook until a knife is easily inserted. Drain them, and when they are at room temperature cut them into small wedges or slices. Toss them into the salad bowl along with the cherry tomatoes and basil leaves. Allow to marinate at room temperature several hours before serving.

Penne al Coccio
Penne with Butter and Truffle Paste

SERVES 4

Of the shorter cuts of pasta, penne is preferred in Tuscany, and there are many recipes for easy sauces to accompany it. *Penne al Coccio is a favorite, usually made in a cast iron stove-top-to-table pan. I made this in Ralph Conte's seaside Tuscan villa kitchen and he loved it so much that he asked if it could be a special on his restaurant menu. This is a very rich first course; the sauce is made from cream, butter, and truffle paste, all the elements for a company dish. Truffle paste is available in Italian speciality stores or on the World Wide Web.*

Put the mushrooms in a dish and cover them with warm water; allow them to plump up for 25 to 30 minutes. Drain them, coarsely chop them, and set aside.

Melt the butter over medium heat in a large earthenware, enameled, cast-iron, or stainless-steel sauté pan. Stir in the prosciutto and allow it to brown slightly. Stir in the mushrooms, salt, and pepper and allow the mixture to cook for 3 or 4 minutes. Stir in the truffle paste and peas. Cover the pan and keep it warm over low heat.

Cook the penne al dente in 4 quarts of boiling water to which 1 tablespoon of salt has been added. Drain the penne.

Over very low heat, stir the cream and half of the cheese into the prosciutto mixture. The sauce should be creamy. Stir in the penne. Serve the penne directly from the pan. Pass the remaining cheese to sprinkle on top, along with a grinding of black pepper.

½ ounce dried porcini mushrooms

4 tablespoons unsalted butter

¼ pound thin-sliced prosciutto, minced

¼ teaspoon fine sea salt

Coarse black pepper to taste

1 teaspoon black truffle paste

1 cup fresh peas

1 pound penne

1 cup heavy cream

4 ounces grated Parmigiano-Reggiano cheese

Zuccotto

Pastry Cream and Fruit–Filled Sponge Cake

SERVES 10

2 cups whole milk

1 tablespoon vanilla extract

4 large egg yolks

¼ cup unbleached all-purpose flour

½ cup sugar

2 tablespoons brandy

1 teaspoon water

1 tablespoon sugar

¾ pound (about 30) ladyfingers

1¾ cups heavy cream, whipped to firm peaks

¾ cup sliced strawberries

8 ounces bittersweet chocolate, chopped medium-fine

Extra chocolate for making curls

Confectioner's sugar for sprinkling

This molded and richly layered pastry cream–filled dessert is said to resemble the dome of Florence's great cathedral and the skull-caps that cardinals wear. And as the cathedral was built in stages, so, too, can zuccotto be made. Make the pastry cream and chop the chocolate several days ahead. Once the zuccotto is assembled it will need to be refrigerated overnight before the finishing touches of whipped cream and chocolate curls are added. Be sure to use good-quality, hard Italian ladyfingers (savoiardi), *not the spongy type found in grocery stores. Most Italian speciality stores carry them.*

For the pastry cream, bring the milk to a boil in a saucepan over medium heat. Remove the pan from the heat and stir in the vanilla. Set aside to cool slightly.

In the top of a double boiler off the heat, whisk the egg yolks. Slowly whisk in the flour, then the milk. Return the double boiler to the heat and cook, stirring constantly with a wooden spoon until the cream thickens and coats the spoon. Stir in the sugar. Pour the pastry cream into a bowl and cover with a piece of buttered waxed paper, pressing it against the surface of the cream. Refrigerate overnight, or several days ahead of assembling the cake.

Line an 8¾ × 4¼-inch glass bowl with plastic wrap, allowing several inches to hang over the sides of the bowl. Fill a spritzer with the brandy, water, and sugar and use it to spray the ladyfingers as you construct the cake.

Start lining the sides of the bowl with sprayed ladyfingers, standing them up lengthwise and making sure the tops of the ladyfingers are even with the rim of the bowl; if they are not, trim them with a knife. Use a couple of broken-up ladyfingers to line the bottom of the bowl.

Carefully spread a layer of pastry cream over the ladyfingers in the bottom of the bowl. Spread about 3 tablespoons of whipped cream over the pastry cream. Arrange a layer of ladyfingers over the whipped cream and spray with the brandy mixture. Spread about ⅔ cup of the pastry cream over the ladyfingers. Arrange the strawberries over the pastry cream, pressing them gently into the cream. Sprinkle half of the chocolate over the strawberries.

Cover the chocolate with another layer of ladyfingers, and spray with the brandy mixture. Spread the remaining pastry cream over the ladyfingers and sprinkle the remaining chocolate over the pastry cream. Spread the remaining whipped cream over the chocolate.

Add a final layer of ladyfingers, covering the filling completely, and spray again with the brandy mixture. Bring the overhanging edges of the plastic wrap up over the top of the cake, pressing down gently on the cake with your hand. Refrigerate overnight.

To unmold, unwrap the top of the cake. Place a serving dish over the top and invert the mold. Carefully remove the plastic wrap from the cake. Sprinkle the cake top with confectioner's sugar to serve. Or whip additional cream and use a pastry bag with a star tip to make a decorative border around the base and top of the cake. Use a vegetable peeler to make chocolate curls from a block of chocolate and sprinkle them over the cream border. Serve immediately.

Minding My Garden

Aglio sott'Aceto (Garlic in Vinegar)

Cippoline sott'Aceto
(Small Onions in Vinegar)

Erbe Toscane (Tuscan Herb Rub)

Insalata di Pomodori Verdi
(Marinated Green Tomato Salad)

Misticanza (Mixed Greens Salad)

Panzanella (Summer Bread Salad)

Pappa al Pomodoro (Tomato Bread Soup)

Passato di Peperoni Gialli
(Cibreo's Yellow Pepper Soup)

Zuppa di Cipolle (Onion Soup)

Scarola e Fagioli (Escarole and Beans)

Scarpaccia Viareggina
(Zucchini Tart Viareggio Style)

Torta di Verdure Verdi
(Crustless Green Vegetable Pie)

Ribollita
(Tuscan Black Cabbage Soup)

PERFECT TIMING! I returned from Tuscany just as planting season was under way at home, and I could not wait to get into my garden and incorporate some of the things I had learned from Tergo, the wise head gardener at Spannocchia, and from his farmhands. My mind was whirling with images of the gorgeous vegetables I had eaten, which my hands were eager to plant. I got right to work putting in *cavolo nero* (black cabbage), so important for making *ribollita* (p. 210), and a serious amount of lettuce seedlings, since every meal ends with a salad in the Esposito house. Lettuces take up one-third of the garden space. One year my husband Guy and I planted over two dozen lettuce types, including *misticanza* (mesculin), *escarole, quattro stagioni, Rossa di Trento,* and *romagna.* We consume huge bowlfuls every day, and I give bouquets of it away to appreciative neighbors.

Traditionally, salad, or *insalata,* is served after the main meal; this practice has to do with the belief that eating salad greens last helps digestion. Guy oversees the *Ciao Italia* garden, and is very picky about how vegetables, especially lettuce, should be harvested. I tend to yank lettuce plants out of the ground; he uses a knife to cut them at the base, which allows for more to grow. As he picks off the leaves they are placed in a large plastic basin of water to keep them from wilting. They are brought into the kitchen, cleaned, soaked, and spun dry in a salad spinner. The leaves are wrapped in paper towels and put into plastic bags.

It always saddens me when the really hot weather arrives, because lettuce is a cool-weather crop and just wilts in the heat. When mid-August arrives, though,

The lettuce patch has so many varieties from which to choose.

there is hope, because a second crop of lettuce can be planted as the days and nights become cooler. Lettuce is on the table well into October, before we must succumb to the grocery store varieties that are water-misted to death to keep them looking fresh.

During the hot summer months in Italy, a hefty salad-like *panzanella* (p. 203) becomes a meal, since garden vegetables are at their peak. Italian salads are dressed simply with extra-virgin olive oil, salt, and either good red wine vinegar or lemon juice. No croutons, please! Friends in Italy have taught me the proper way to dress a salad. Pour the oil into a large serving spoon and drizzle it over the salad greens before tossing them. This coats the leaves so they will not wilt. Then add the salt to the serving spoon and pour the vinegar or lemon juice over the salt. Use a smaller spoon to stir and completely dissolve the salt, then pour it over the greens and toss well. It is important to use a salad bowl that's deep enough to allow sufficient tossing without the lettuce spilling out of the bowl.

Tomatoes are another crop that there is just too much of in my garden, but we cannot help ourselves when we think that it is a long time from the end of September to the next tasty tomato that will pass our lips in early August. In Italy, *pomodorini*, or cherry tomatoes, are strung up and hung to dry for winter use. I preserve mine by drying them in a dehydrator or freezing them whole right from the vine in plastic bags. In the winter months they are a taste of summer in soups, stews, and stocks.

At the sign of the first frost all the unripened tomatoes are harvested and placed under layers of newspaper where they ripen slowly. And, of course, green ones are used in salads (*insalata di pomodori verdi*, p. 201). Tergo would be pleased.

One of the most interesting things I learned in Tuscany was the technique of allowing squash vines to grow vertically, climbing up a rope or string against a fence or post. This saves a lot of room, and it makes the zucchini visible without your having to crouch and look under gigantic leaves to see if it has grown so large that the only destination for it is not the soup pot but the compost heap.

What is Tuscan cooking—or any Italian cooking—without herbs? Sage (*salvia*) is the most popular herb in Tuscany, along with basil, parsley, and rosemary. Only Siena prefers tarragon (*dragoncello)* in some of its dishes. Sage is said to impart wisdom and has been used since ancient times; its pungent taste is a perfect compliment to Tuscany's earthy meat and poultry dishes. In fact, herbs are used in Tuscan dishes more than salt and pepper. And because herbs are perennials, they are a hopeful reminder that with tender care they will keep coming back year after year—maybe not as lush as the thick bushes in Tergo's garden, but sturdy enough to provide my kitchen with what I need.

When I am minding my garden I think of all that I learned at Spannocchia. I am a better gardener for the experience.

Aglio sott'Aceto
Garlic in Vinegar

MAKES 4 ONE-QUART BOTTLES

2 or 3 bulbs of fresh garlic, separated into cloves, peeled, and left whole

Fresh whole basil leaves, washed, stemmed, and wiped dry

Whole peppercorns

Whole coriander seeds

Coarse kosher salt

1 gallon white cider or white wine vinegar

4 one-quart bottles

Vinegar has a symbolic meaning for Italians. They use the phrase "un segreto dell'aceto" (a vinegar secret) to mean keeping a secret. The implication is that when you have a taste of vinegar, it is difficult to talk, and the secret is safe.

*I*mmersing fresh garlic cloves in good vinegar makes them milder in flavor, and good to use when you want just a whiff of garlic in a dish, not a pungent presence. The success of this preparation depends on using garlic that is not too old. Look for tight knobs with no splits, soft spots, or sprouts growing from the knob. Garlic grown in home gardens is best cured after harvesting, which means to tie the bunches together and hang them in a dry, dark place until the papers crackle. This vinegar and garlic combination will be ready to use in four weeks. In Tuscany, garlic-flavored vinegar is used with boiled meats.

Use dark bottles to prevent light from turning the garlic dark. Make as many as you like, putting at least 6 garlic cloves in each bottle with 2 to 4 fresh basil leaves, 8 to 10 peppercorns, 1 teaspoon of coriander seeds, and 1 teaspoon of salt. Fill to the top with the vinegar and cap. Shake the bottles occasionally; store in a cool, dark spot. The vinegar is ready to use in 4 weeks. Use smaller decorative bottles to make a larger quantity. Use the vinegar to sprinkle on boiled meats, in potato salads and green salads, vegetable dishes, and for deglazing pans.

Cipolline sott'Aceto
Small Onions in Vinegar

Onions—red ones, white ones, yellow ones, and the flat ones called cipolline—are always in my garden, and are ready for harvesting when the tops flop over and turn brown. I harvest and dry them in my garden shed until the onion papers are brittle, then store them in mesh bags in a dark, not cold area. I could not cook without onions, and I often marinate them in vinegar and spices to use as a condiment with meats, poultry, or fish, or for dressing up a dull salad. I have even added them to fruit salads. In a pretty jar they make a great hostess gift.

In a nonaluminum saucepan, boil the vinegar with all the ingredients except the onions for 3 or 4 minutes.

With a knife, make a small "x" in each onion and add them to the vinegar mixture and cook for 2 minutes. Turn off the heat and allow the onions to steep covered in the vinegar for several hours.

Transfer the onions and the vinegar mixture to a jar, cap, and store in the refrigerator. They will keep for a month.

2 cups red wine vinegar

2 whole bay leaves

1 tablespoon whole black peppercorns

1 teaspoon whole cloves

2 sprigs fresh thyme

One 2-inch piece cinnamon stick

1 teaspoon coarse salt

1 pound boiling onions, peeled and left whole

Erbe Toscane
Tuscan Herb Rub

2 cups rosemary needles

1 cup sage leaves

4 large cloves garlic

2 teaspoons coarse salt
(kosher is best)

One of the things I have learned in Tuscan kitchens I have visited is that one must always have a jar of erbe toscane (Tuscan herbs) on hand for rubbing into roasts and using for general cooking. The most favored herbs are rosemary, sage, and garlic. This is a great way to make use of the herbs in your garden.

Make a pile of the rosemary, sage, garlic, and salt on a cutting board. Use a chef's knife or a *mezzaluna* (rocking knife) and mince the ingredients. Spread the mixture on the cutting board or on paper towels and allow it to dry overnight.

Transfer the mixture to a jar and keep it in the refrigerator.

Use it to rub on pork roasts or chicken, or mix it into sautéing vegetables and into soups. It makes a great little culinary gift, too.

Vary the herbs and add others, like thyme, fennel seeds or fennel pollen, and even lemon zest.

Insalata di Pomodori Verdi
Marinated Green Tomato Salad

SERVES 4

Plump, radiant red tomatoes are showstoppers in the mercati (markets) of Italy. But it might surprise you to know that Italians like their salad tomatoes on the greenish side since they are firmer and hold up well. Riper tomatoes are reserved for making sauces. Make this salad early in the day, then serve it for lunch or dinner, and mop up the flavorful juices with slices of crusty Tuscan bread. Even though it is not traditional, I like to add shavings of pecorino cheese to the salad for added interest.

Mix all the ingredients except the tomatoes in a large bowl. Add the tomato slices and toss gently with your hands. Layer the slices in a platter, slightly overlapping them. Cover and allow the salad to marinate at room temperature for several hours before serving. When ready to serve, sprinkle the cheese over the top.

½ cup extra-virgin olive oil

1 clove garlic, finely minced

2 tablespoons minced fresh oregano, or 1½ teaspoons dried

1 teaspoon fine sea salt

¼ cup red wine vinegar

¼ teaspoon sugar

3 or 4 meaty green tomatoes, thinly sliced

Shavings of pecorino cheese with peppercorns

Misticanza
Mixed Greens Salad

SERVES 4

DRESSING

⅓ cup extra-virgin olive oil

¾ teaspoon fine sea salt

3 tablespoons red wine vinegar or fresh lemon juice

SALAD

1 cup washed and dried chicory leaves

1 cup washed and dried escarole leaves

1 cup washed and dried dandelion greens

1 cup washed and dried radicchio leaves

An Italian mixed greens salad is not likely to include iceberg lettuce, known in Italy as crocantine or Braziliana. *Rather, the salad bowl is filled with a delightful mixture of bitter greens, including chicory, escarole, dandelion greens, and crunchy radicchio—and is anything but boring. It is a work of edible art, a refreshing wake-up call for the palate, and a reminder that Italians know how to enjoy the bitter with the sweet.*

Mix the salad dressing ingredients in a jar and set aside.

Toss the greens together in a large salad bowl. Pour the dressing over the greens and toss well.

Panzanella
Summer Bread Salad

SERVES 6

Panzanella *means "bread in a swamp," and is a summer salad that is popular all over Italy. In Tuscany this was originally a country dish eaten for breakfast or as a snack. Tomatoes, onions, and cucumbers make up the dish, as well as stale bread that is moistened in water or vinegar and extra-virgin olive oil. I cannot stress enough that the quality of the bread is critical. Make this salad early in the day and hold it at room temperature so all the flavors can mingle and the bread becomes permeated with the juice of the tomatoes.*

Combine the tomatoes in a small bowl with the sugar and set aside.

Tear the bread into chunks and dip them quickly into a bowl of room-temperature water. Squeeze the water out and crumble the bread into a salad bowl. Add the tomatoes, onion, cucumber, parsley, and basil and toss gently.

Pour the dressing over the salad and toss again. Cover the salad and allow it to sit at room temperature for several hours.

Just before serving toss the salad gently.

1 cup coarsely chopped plum or cherry tomatoes

1 teaspoon sugar

6 thick slices stale bread, crust removed

½ cup thinly sliced Spanish onion

1 cup seeded and diced cucumber

¼ cup minced fresh parsley

2 large basil leaves, torn into pieces

DRESSING

6 tablespoons extra-virgin olive oil

3 tablespoons red wine vinegar

2 cloves garlic, minced

½ to 1 teaspoon fine sea salt

Pappa al Pomodoro
Tomato Bread Soup

MAKES 8 SERVINGS

2½ pounds plum
tomatoes, cored
and cut in half

½ cup extra-virgin
olive oil

½ pound leeks,
white bulb only,
finely diced

12 basil leaves, minced

3 cups hot chicken or
vegetable broth,
fresh or canned

¾ teaspoon fine sea salt

Coarse black pepper
to taste

3 cups stale bread, cut
into 1-inch cubes

Pappa al pomodoro *is not easy to describe; it is a thick, soupy tomato mixture. It is an old-fashioned country dish that, like many other Tuscan soups, has bread as a component. The secret here is to use meaty, juicy plum tomatoes at their peak, and good, coarse day-old bread. This is one of the ways that I like to use up summer tomatoes.*

Puree the tomatoes in a food processor until smooth. Pour the mixture into a fine sieve placed over a large bowl. Strain the liquid with a wooden spoon and discard the seeds and skins. Set aside.

Heat ¼ cup of the olive oil in a large soup pot, stir in the leeks and half of the basil, and cook until the leeks soften. Stir in the tomato liquid, broth, salt, and pepper and cook over medium heat for 5 minutes. Keep the soup covered off the heat.

Heat the remaining olive oil in a large sauté pan. Stir in the remaining basil and the bread cubes. Brown the bread quickly over medium heat. Stir the cubes into the soup. Cover the pan and allow the bread to absorb the liquid.

When ready to serve slowly reheat the soup.

Pass extra-virgin olive oil to drizzle on top.

Passato di Peperoni Gialli
Cibreo's Yellow Pepper Soup

SERVES 6 TO 8

*C*ibreo is a fabulous restaurant in Florence where I have had some really scrumptious meals. One of my favorite recipes from their kitchen is this colorful, pureed yellow pepper soup. It is all warmth and sunshine on a dreary winter's day. I like to add a twist and surprise my guests with a thin layer of spinach puree in the bottom of the bowl.

Cook the spinach in a large soup pot with no additional water just until it is wilted. Drain it and partially squeeze it dry. Transfer the spinach to a food processor and puree it with the milk or heavy cream. The puree should not be too thick, but more like the consistency of fruit sauce. Stir in the nutmeg and keep the spinach warm. This step can be done two days ahead and refrigerated. Reheat it when ready to serve the soup.

Finely mince the carrot, onion, and celery together and cook them in the olive oil in a small sauté pan until they are very soft. Set aside.

Put the peppers and potatoes in the same pot used to cook the spinach. Cover them with the broth. Cook covered until very soft, about 25 minutes. Transfer the mixture to a food processor, in batches, along with the carrot mixture, and puree until smooth. Transfer the mixture back to the soup pot and stir in the salt and lemon juice. If the soup seems too thick, thin it down with a little milk.

When ready to serve, reheat the spinach sauce and spoon a thin layer of it in the base of individual soup bowls. Carefully ladle the soup over the spinach and garnish with fried bread crutons if desired. Or cut out some shapes from raw red pepper with a canapé cutter and float on top of the soup.

1 pound spinach, washed and stemmed (drain but leave some water clinging to leaves)

1 tablespoon milk or heavy cream

¼ teaspoon nutmeg

1 carrot, coarsely chopped

1 red onion, coarsely chopped

1 stalk celery, coarsely chopped

3 tablespoons extra-virgin olive oil

3 meaty yellow peppers (about 1¾ pounds), seeded and cut into strips

3 medium Yukon Gold potatoes, peeled and cut into chunks

6 cups hot vegetable broth

1½ teaspoons fine sea salt

2 tablespoons fresh lemon juice

Zuppa di Cipolle
Onion Soup

SERVES 4

6 tablespoons extra-virgin olive oil

¼ pound pancetta, diced

5 large yellow onions, peeled and thinly sliced

¼ cup fresh lemon juice

5½ cups hot low-sodium beef broth, fresh or canned

½ cup dry red wine

Fine sea salt to taste

Coarse black pepper to taste

4 slices coarse bread cut ½-inch thick

1 cup grated Parmigiano-Reggiano cheese

Tuscan cooks are partial to making soups, and, like pasta, they make them a first course or a main course, depending on the number of ingredients. Bread is often a component in Tuscan soup, either as a thickener, as in Pappa al Pomodoro (p. 204), or placed in the base of a soup bowl. I make this hearty soup using a variety of onions from my garden, but common yellow onions yield a very nice flavor.

In a large soup pot, heat 4 tablespoons of the oil over medium-high heat, add the pancetta, and cook for 2 minutes. Stir in the onions, cover the pot, and cook slowly for about 15 minutes, stirring often. When the onions are limp add the lemon juice and allow it to evaporate.

Pour in the broth and wine. Stir the mixture. Cover the pot and simmer for 30 minutes. Add salt and pepper to taste. Keep the soup warm while you fry the bread.

Preheat the broiler.

Heat the remaining olive oil in a sauté pan and brown the bread on both sides. Drain the slices on paper towels, then place a slice in each of 4 individual ovenproof soup bowls. Pour the soup over the bread and divide and sprinkle the cheese over the top.

Broil the soup until the cheese melts. Serve immediately.

NOTE: You will need ovenproof soup bowls or large ramekins for this dish.

Scarola e Fagioli
Escarole and Beans

SERVES 4

Creamy, white cannellini beans are everywhere in Tuscan cooking. Made into smooth spreads for crostini, stuffed into vegetables, pureed into soups, and added as fillers for salads, this bean is king in Tuscan kitchens. Scarola e fagioli (escarole and beans) is an old recipe, once considered a poor dish, that now finds its way on the menus of upscale restaurants. Use dried white kidney, Great Northern, or borlotti beans for this energy-packed dish.

Soak the beans overnight covered with water. The next day, drain the beans, put them in a pot, cover with water, and cook them until the skins slip off easily when pressed between your fingers. Drain the beans and set aside.

Put the escarole in a large sauté pan, cover the pan, and wilt the leaves over low heat. Drain the escarole and squeeze out most of the water. Coarsely chop it and set it aside.

In the same sauté pan, heat the olive oil, add the onions, and cook them over medium heat until they are very soft. Stir in the garlic, red pepper flakes, salt, pepper, and the escarole, and continue to cook for 3 or 4 minutes. Stir in the olives and the beans. Serve hot as an accompaniment to meat or fish, or serve as an antipasto over slices of toasted bread.

½ cup dried white kidney beans

1 head escarole (about 1¼ pounds), leaves separated and well-washed

⅓ cup extra-virgin olive oil

1 small red onion, thinly sliced

2 cloves garlic, minced

½ teaspoon hot red pepper flakes

½ teaspoon fine sea salt

Coarse black pepper to taste

8 oil-cured black olives, pitted and minced

Toasted bread slices (optional)

Scarpaccia Viareggina
Zucchini Tart Viareggio Style

SERVES 8

1 pound small zucchini

4 tablespoons unsalted
butter, melted

½ cup sugar

1 tablespoon
vanilla extract

¾ cup milk

½ teaspoon salt

1 cup unbleached
all-purpose flour

2 tablespoons
extra-virgin olive oil

Viareggio is a coastal city famous for its Carnivale, *where you might sample* Scarpaccia Viareggina, *a delicious, slightly sweet zucchini tart, and are likely to ask yourself, is it dessert or a savory dish? It can be either; at one time it was served after the meal, but today it is thought of more as a snack food. It takes its name from the word* scarpa *(shoe), because it looks well cooked when taken from the oven, like a well-worn shoe.*

Butter and flour a 9 × 12 × 2½-inch, or 7 × 11-inch baking dish and set it aside.

Cut the zucchini into thin rounds. Layer them in a colander and sprinkle salt between each layer. Place a weight, such as a 28-ounce can of tomatoes, on the zucchini to weigh the slices down. Allow the zucchini to "sweat" for 1 hour. Then rinse and dry the slices and set them aside.

Preheat the oven to 350°F.

In a large bowl, whisk together the butter, sugar, and vanilla until smooth. Stir in the milk, salt, and flour to create a batter. Fold in the zucchini.

Pour the mixture into the baking dish. Drizzle the top with the olive oil.

Bake for 40 minutes, or until a skewer comes out clean when inserted into the center.

Serve warm, cut into squares.

NOTE: Small-size zucchini have less water and fewer seeds, and are more tender than larger ones.

Torta di Verdure Verdi
Crustless Green Vegetable Pie

SERVES 6

From the vegetable gardens of Spannocchia comes this tasty and healthy crustless vegetable pie. It is usually made with a variety of greens, such as spinach, cavolo nero (black cabbage), kale, Swiss chard, zucchini, and broccoli rape. The rule of thumb for cooking tender greens like spinach and Swiss chard is to wash the leaves well, then put them in a soup pot without any additional water. Cover the pot and wilt the greens. This will take about 2 minutes. Drain and squeeze the leaves dry. For sturdy-leaf vegetables like kale, cook the leaves in boiling water until tender.

Butter a 9½ × 1½-inch baking dish and set aside. Preheat the oven to 375°F.

Melt the butter over medium heat in a sauté pan. Stir in the bread crumbs and coat them with the butter, then allow them to brown slightly. Transfer them to a small bowl and set aside.

Chop the greens coarsely and put them in a large bowl. In a separate bowl mix the eggs, besciamella sauce, half-and-half, salt, nutmeg, and pepper. Stir in ¼ cup of the cheese and combine well. Transfer the mixture to the baking dish.

Sprinkle the remaining cheese over the top, then sprinkle the bread crumbs over the cheese.

Bake about 25 minutes, or until the pie is firm and brown around the edges. Serve immediately.

NOTE: 2 pounds of fresh spinach equals 1¾ cups cooked and squeezed; 1 pound of fresh Swiss chard equals 1 cup cooked and squeezed, 1 pound fresh kale equals approximately 2 cups cooked and squeezed.

1 tablespoon unsalted butter

⅔ cup toasted bread crumbs

1¾ cups cooked spinach, coarsely chopped

1 cup cooked Swiss chard, coarsely chopped

1 cup cooked kale, coarsely chopped

3 large eggs

1 cup besciamella sauce (p. 138)

1 cup half-and-half

1 teaspoon fine sea salt

¼ teaspoon fresh ground nutmeg

Coarse black pepper to taste

½ cup grated Parmigiano-Reggiano cheese

Ribollita
Tuscan Black Cabbage Soup

SERVES 8

1 cup dried white beans

2 tablespoons extra-virgin olive oil, plus more for garnish

1 large sprig fresh rosemary

1 medium onion, diced

1 tablespoon fresh chili pepper, diced

4 carrots, diced

2 stalks celergy, diced

2 potatoes, peeled and diced

1 small zucchini, diced

1 pound kale, stemmed, washed, and torn into pieces

6 plum tomatoes, diced

6 cups hot water

1 Parmesan cheese rind (optional)

½ cup green beans, cut into thirds

1½ teaspoons celery salt

1 tablespoon salt

Grinding black pepper

8 slices toasted bread

Ribollita is a classic Tuscan soup. The word means to reboil, as in make this soup one day and reheat it the next. The key ingredients are fresh or dried cannellini beans and cavolo nero *or black cabbage with sturdy dark green elongated leaves. Use kale in place of* cavolo nero. *This hearty soup is usually served over slices of thick toasted bread. Begin the process by soaking the dried beans overnight. I like to add the salt and pepper after the soup is cooked. I also like to add a Parmesan cheese rind to the soup as it cooks but this is optional.*

Put the beans in a bowl and cover them with 3 cups of cold water. Allow them to stand overnight. The following day drain the beans and transfer them to a 2-quart pot. Cover the bean with 6 cups of water and cook them for about 45 minutes or until tender. Drain the beans. Puree half of them and set all the beans aside.

Heat the olive oil in a large soup pot. Add the rosemary, onion, chili pepper, carrots, and celery. Cook over medium heat until the vegetables begin to soften. Stir in the potatoes, zucchini, kale, and tomatoes. Cook 2 minutes. Stir in the whole beans.

Pour in the water and the pureed beans, and stir all the ingredients well. Add the cheese rind if you have one. Cover the pot, reduce the heat to simmer and cook for 25 minutes. Uncover the pot, stir in the green beans and cook 5 more minutes.

Stir in the celery salt, salt, and pepper. Taste for seasoning.

Toast the bread slices then place one in each of 8 soup bowls. Ladle the soup over the bread and serve. Pass additional extra-virgin olive oil to drizzle on top.

A Day for Vin Santo

It was a sad day when the crew and I said *arrivederci* to Tuscany; we all agreed that we could live here very nicely, and it is a dream of mine to do that some day, but for now we must live off our wonderful experience and memories of the days spent filming another season of *Ciao Italia*. Our goal completed, it was time to celebrate, which for me meant a wine toast with Vin Santo—but not just any one; it had to be Avignonese Vin Santo, the best dessert wine in all of Tuscany, as far as I am concerned.

As Ettore Falvo, one of the producers of this exquisite wine, explained to me, Avignonese Vin Santo is made from grechetto, malvasia, toscana, and trebbiano grapes that are left to dry on straw mats, or left hanging in bunches in a consistent-temperature atmosphere, before being crushed and put into small barrels along with some of the "mother" wine from the last fermented barrel. The barrels are sealed and the contents left to age for eight years before being bottled. When opened, the amber-colored sweet wine, with flavors of dried fruits and nuts, should be sipped slowly to savor all of its complexities. The name Vin Santo, or holy wine, comes from the practice of using it during the celebration of the Mass. That may have been common centuries ago, but today its exorbitant price and limited availability prohibit this tradition.

As we toasted the wrap-up of another series with this fruity wine, I recalled the wonderful *pranzo* (lunch) I enjoyed at the winery La Selva with Ettore. Sitting at a long country table in a vaulted-ceiling room with a symphony of rain pouring down outside, the gloom of the day was whisked away as we enjoyed a meal of *prosciutto di cinghiale* (raw-cured wild boar) and *finocchiona*, or Tuscan dried sausage studded with fennel seeds, served with the most perfectly shaped and sweet fresh figs I have ever seen. This was followed by *fegato d'anatra* (duck liver), with a texture as smooth as pudding, and served with a plum sauce. *Sformato di porcini* (small porcini mushroom molds) came next and provided such an earthy flavor that I could see why Tuscan cooks covet their mushrooms. And all this was just the antipasto! Our first course of pasta, *pappardelle,* was served with a rich wild boar sauce, followed by *trippa* (tripe). Small turkey meatballs, *polpettine,* coated in bread crumbs and deep-fried, had a bright taste of fresh lemon. Truly, I had never eaten so much, but I knew there was more to come, and it did come—in the form of fresh *cannellini* beans served at room temperature and mixed with the winery's own peppery olive oil. When the *insalata mista* (mixed salad) was served, I knew this incredible meal was coming to a close. The semiclimax was a chocolate-cream cake served with fresh raspberry puree. And then, the climax itself: Vin Santo. How proudly and reverently it was poured by Ettore. The bouquet of the wine filled the room, and with glasses in hand and a toast of *"salute,"* we settled back and let the wine speak for itself.

In the four hours that I lingered at table with Ettore, I tasted most of the major foods that define *la cucina povera,* Tuscany's culinary traditions, culminating with a world-class dessert wine. Sipping it and watching the crew enjoy it, too, I knew that on this journey to Tuscany we had captured the essence of those traditions.

The Tuscan Pantry

Many of the recipes in this book can be made in short order with staples already on hand in the pantry or the refrigerator. A well-stocked pantry is key to always being ready for meal preparation, and my rule is to buy several of each item to avoid running out of ingredients. Specialty items can also be found on food-related Web sites, or from mail-order sources (see p.219).

DRY AND JARRED STAPLES

Tuscan olive oils

Dried *cannellini* beans, chickpeas, and
  lentils

Unbleached all-purpose flour

Whole wheat flour

Potato starch

Dried yeast

Dried pasta, including *pappardelle,*
  penne, and tagliatelle

Red wine vinegar

Dry red and white wines for cooking,
  not cooking wine

Currants

Raisins

Cinnamon

Cloves

Nutmeg

Ginger, ground

Whole black peppercorns

Bay leaves

Capers in salt

Walnuts, almonds, pine nuts,
  hazelnuts

Vanilla and almond extracts

Honey

Candied orange and lemon rinds

Candied citron

Rice papers (*ostia*)

Fine and coarse sea salt

Coarse black pepper

Red pepper flakes

Anchovies in olive oil

Tuna in olive oil

Confectioner's sugar

Granulated sugar

Arborio rice
Low-sodium chicken, vegetable, and
  beef broths
Chicken, vegetable, and beef bouillon
  cubes

DAIRY

Eggs, large
Mascarpone cheese
Mozzarella cheese
Parmigiano-Reggiano cheese
Pecorino cheese
Pecorino cheese with black
  peppercorns
Ricotta cheese
Unsalted butter

MEAT PRODUCTS AND
CURED MEATS

Pancetta (Italian Bacon)
Prosciutto crudo
Soppressata

VEGETABLES AND HERBS

Onions
Shallots

Scallions
Garlic
Celery
Carrots
Canned plum tomatoes
Fresh plum tomatoes
Fresh cherry tomatoes
Dried tomatoes in olive oil
Fresh mushrooms
Dried porcini mushrooms
Fennel
Red potatoes
Italian flat-leaf parsley
Fresh sage
Fresh rosemary
Fresh tarragon
Fresh basil
Fresh mint
Spinach
Chicory
Arugula
Beets
Beet greens
Kale
Cabbage

Favorite Tuscan Restaurants

This is a short list of Tuscan favorites that I recommend to anyone traveling to Tuscany.

CORTONA

II Falconiere
San Martino a Bocena
Phone 055 612 616

A well-appointed restaurant serving traditional dishes, including homemade pasta, grilled meats, and fabulous desserts. Reservations recommended.

FLORENCE

Cantinetta Antinori
Piazza Antinori 3
Phone 055 292 234

A beautifully appointed *palazzo* belonging to the wine-producing Antinori family; a good menu featuring Tuscan specialties and a superb wine list. Reservations recommended.

Casa Anita
Via del Pariascio 2 R.
Phone 055 218 698

This small rustic restaurant features Tuscan specialties, grilled meats, and good pasta dishes.

Cibreo
Via de Macci
Phone 055 234 1100

Typical Florentine dishes, including tripe, lamb with artichokes, duck, and delicious soups. No pasta is served here. Reservations recommended.

Coco Lezzone
Via Parioncino 26
Phone 055 287 178

Hearty, traditional cooking, including *baccala* and tripe, *pappa al pomodoro,* and *ribollita. Bistecca,* a specialty, is huge and served rare. No reservations taken.

Da Benvenuto
Via Mosca 16
Phone 055 213 619

One of the most authentic restaurants in the city, and reasonably priced. Specialties include *ribollita,* tripe, and typical pasta dishes. A place filled with noise and local charm.

Da Pennello
Via Dante Alighieri 4
Phone 055 294 848

A very busy osteria serving full-course meals as well as lighter fare from an outstanding antipasto bar. Definitely make reservations.

Trattoria Garga
Via del Moro 48
Phone 055 239 8898

One of the most popular restaurants in Florence. Fresh, homemade tagliatelle, very tasty risotto, and beautifully prepared salads are hallmarks of this establishment. Be sure to reserve a table at least a day ahead.

LUCCA

Solferino
Via delle Gavine 50
San Macario in Piano
Phone 058 359 118

A family-run restaurant with a great reputation. Menu is mainly Tuscan favorites. Reservations recommended.

MONTALCINO

Ristorante Banfi
Castello Poggio alle Mura
Loc. San Angelo Scalo
Phone 577 840 111

Traditional Tuscan dishes served in the winery's fabulous restaurant. Wild boar, *pinci*, and typical bean dishes.

PIENZA

Club 11 Rossellino
Piazza di Spagna 4
Phone 578 758 286

Medium-priced traditional dishes including wild boar, *pappardelle,* and bean dishes.

PISA

Al Ristoro del Vecchi Macelli
Via Volturno 49
Phone 050 204 24

Traditional bean dishes, fish and game specialties. Wonderful desserts. Reservations recommended.

PRATO

Osvaldo Baroncelli
Via Fra Bartolomeo 13
Phone 055 574 238

Elegant food with a twist, like small tarts with potato and porcini mushrooms, and chicken stuffed with pistachios. Delicious breads. Reservations recommended.

SAN SEPOLCRO

Da Ventura
Via Aggiunti 30
Phone 575 742 560

One of my favorites for the most delicious roasted pork and veal you will ever eat. The antipasto table is wonderfully fresh and all the pasta is made by hand. Not to be missed. Reservations are necessary.

SETTIGNANO

La Sosta del Rossellino
Via del Rossellino 2r
Phone 055 697 245

This wonderful wine bar *(enoteca)* serves delicious homemade pasta and gnocchi, as well as an outstanding *carpaccio di maiale* (raw-cured pork). The wines are exquisite as are the selection of cheeses. Try the tagliatelle with orange and lemon sauce. One of my favorites. Reservations a must.

SIENA

Antica Trattoria Popei
Piazza del Mercato 6
Phone 057 280 894

Typical Tuscan and Sienese dishes are well prepared in this homey trattoria that can be a bit noisy. Reservations recommended.

Ai Marsili
Via del Castoro 3
Phone 057 747 154

Beautifully appointed restaurant with a great wine cellar; typical Tuscan dishes. Reservations recommended.

Mail-Order Sources

You may find this list handy for items that are not available in grocery or specialty food stores.

Ciao Times
PO Box 891
Durham, New Hampshire 03824
www.ciaoitalia.com

Ciao Italia-related products, including personalized aprons.

Claudio's King of Cheese
929 South Ninth Street
South Philadelphia, Pennsylvania 19147

Tuscan olive oils, wide variety of dried pasta, including *pappardelle,* tagliatelle, and penne. Cheeses from most regions of Italy, including Tuscan pecorino and pecorino with peppercorns.

Colavita USA
2537 Brunswick Avenue
Linden, New Jersey 07036
www.colavita.com

Penne, *pappardelle,* canned tomatoes, vinegars, olive oil, and speciality food baskets.

Coluccio and Sons
1214 60th Street
Brooklyn, New York 11219

A complete Italian grocery store carrying a wide variety of imported Italian food-stuffs from dried beans and lentils to olive oils, cheeses, and cured meats.

Dean & Deluca
Catalog Orders
PO Box 20810
Wichita, Kansas 67208-6810
www.deanandeluca.com

Cookware, Italian meats, cheeses, and spices.

DiBruno Brothers
109 South 18th Street
Philadelphia, Pennsylvania 19103
(215) 665-9220 (Catalog)

Cured meats, pancetta, cheeses, olive oils, pasta, anchovies, and capers in salt.

Fante's
1006 South 9th Street
Philadelphia, Pennsylvania 19147
(800) 878-5557
www.fantes.com

Large selection of baking needs, *ostia* (rice papers), and cookware.

Gallucci's Italian Foods
6610 Euclid Avenue
Cleveland, Ohio 44103
(216) 881-0045 (Catalog)

A wide variety of cheeses, cured meats, olive oils, wines, pasta, flours, nuts, flavorings, olives, and much more. An all-encompassing Italian supermarket.

Joe Pace and Sons
335 Main Street

Saugus, Massachusetts 02113
(781) 231-9599

Quality meats and provisions; well-stocked grocery store, Italian seeds, bakery, wide line of olive oils, pasta, nuts, spices, and vinegars.

King Arthur Flour
PO Box 1010
Norwich, Vermont 05055
(802) 649-3881 or (800) 827-6836 (Baker's Catalog)
www.kingarthurflour.com

A baker's dream of a store; all types of flour, including Italian flour, dried yeast, extracts, bakeware, nuts, chocolate, and sugars.

Kitchen Etc.
32 Industrial Drive
Exeter, New Hampshire 03833
(800) 232-4070 (Catalog)
www.kitchenetc.com

A full line of bake and cookware, small appliances, pasta machines, kitchen tools, dinnerware, table linens, cutlery, and cookbooks.

Seeds From Italy
PO Box 149
Winchester, Massachusetts 01890 (Catalog)
www.growitalian.com

A fabulous source for vegetable- and flower-garden seeds from Italy.

The Spice Corner
904 South Ninth Street
Philadelphia, Pennsylvania 19147
(800) SPICES or (215) 925-1661
www.thespicecorner.com

Unique selection of dried herbs and spices.

Venda Ravioli Company
265 Atwells Avenue

Providence, Rhode Island 02903
(401) 421-9105
www.vendaravioli.com

Full line of imported Italian food products, including some of the finest Tuscan olive oils, Tuscan ceramic ware, complete deli department, fresh breads, rolls, full line of imported Tuscan cheeses, olives, capers, packaged cookies, homemade filled pasta.

Zabar's
2245 Broadway
New York, New York 10024
(212) 787-2000 or (800) 697-6301 (Catalog)
www.zabars.com

Good source for Italian cheeses, cured meats, olive oils, and cookware.

Bob's Red Mill Natural Foods, Inc.
5209 S.E. International Way
Milwaukie, Oregon 97222
(800) 349-2173
www.bobsredmill.com

This is a great source for organic whole grains, pastry, semolina, spelt, and other flours, cereals, beans, seeds, baking supplies, gluten-free products, and cookbooks.

Tuscan Food and Wine Web Sites

www.firenze.net/events/winefood.htm
Information about traditional recipes and food excursions in Tuscany.

www.castellobanfi.com
Information on the Banfi winery, as well as recipes, restaurant news, and links to Michelin-starred restaurants.

www.foodandwine.com
Wine and food experts share advice.

www.enotecarossellino.com
Information about the restaurant La Sosta del Rossellino, as well as news on upcoming wine events.

www.famigliamartelli.it
Family-run pasta company near Pisa making some of the best dried pastas, including penne, *maccheroni, spaghettini,* and spaghetti. Martelli pasta can be found in the United States in specialty food stores and in Italian markets.

www.knowital.com
General information on foods and wines of Tuscany and Italy.

www.simpleinternet.com
Recipes and a dictionary of wines.

www.theitalianecookbook.com
A site devoted to all the recipes that belong to traditional Italian cooking.

www.tuscan-foodstuffs.com
Wide variety of food products typical of Tuscany. Catalog.

www.tuscanfarm.com
Wines, cheeses, and typical Tuscan food products, including olive oils and spices.

www.agferrari-foods.com
Variety of Tuscan foods, and general Italian food items.

www.seeds@growitalian.com
A site devoted to Italian seeds.

English Index

Page numbers of illustrations appear in *italics*.

Almond(s), 48
   Cookies, 49–50
   Siena-Style, Cookies, 178–79
Anise, Raisin-, Bread, 67
Antipasto, 61
   crostini, 94
   Escarole and Beans, 207
   Iris's Tuscan Meatballs, 77–78
   Leek Tart, 12–13
   Little Black Toasts with Chicken Liver
      Spread, 99
   Little Diced Tomato and Herb Toasts,
      98
   Nancy's Tuna and Olive Spread,
      100
   Olive Pizza, 31
   Pecorino with Black Peppercorns in
      Olive Oil, 152
   Salted Pizza Bites, 175
Apple(s)
   Cake, 126–27
   Fried, Rings, 127
   with Raspberry Sauce, 140
   Stuffed Figs Davanzati Style,
      87
Artichokes, 8, 135
   Braised, 10
Arugula
   with beefsteak, 40
   Iris's Tuscan Meatballs, 77–78

Bartolo, Taddeo di, 34
Basil
   Cherry Tomato–Pesto Sauce, 43
   keeping leaves green, 41
   Penne with Uncooked Tomato-Olive
      Sauce, 160
   Pesto, 41
   Tomato Bread Soup, 204
Beans, 8–9, 72
   Cooked in a Flask, 74
   Escarole and, 207
   Grilled Eggplant and Green, Salad,
      187
   Iris's Pasta Fantasia with Fresh, and
      Olive Sauce, 80
   pasta used with, 72
   Pecorino Cheese and Fava, 154
   Soup for the Lombards, 81
   Stewed, 75
   Tuscan Black Cabbage Soup, 210
Beef
   bistecca, 38, 40, 60, 134
   Grilled T-Bone Steak, *38*, 40
   Iris's Tuscan Meatballs, 77–78
   Lulu San Angelo's Ricotta Cheese
      Meatballs, 79
   rub for grilling (*battuto*), 38
   Stuffed Zucchini with Ginger, 139
   Tuscan, Stew, 123
Berti, Luciano and Anna, 134–35

Biscottificio Antonio Mattei,
      48–49
Braised Artichokes, 10
Bread
   baking, 95, 97
   Bruschetta, Pesto on, 41
   Buccellato with Strawberries and
      Mascarpone, 68
   Grape Harvest, 124–25
   grilled, xvii, 31, 61, 92
   home-made, 93
   Little Cubed, Sauce, 121
   Little Diced Tomato and Herb Toasts,
      98
   loaves, shape of, 93
   Nancy's Tuscan, 96–97
   Onion Soup, 206
   Raisin-Anise, 67
   in sauce, 92, 118
   in soup, 92, 206
   starter dough, 92, 94, 96
   as stuffing, 92
   Summer, Salad, 203
   Tomato, Soup, 204
   Tuscan, 94–95
   Tuscan Black Cabbage Soup, 210
   wheat for, 92
   with vegetables, 92
Buccellato with Strawberries and
      Mascarpone, 68

Cabbage, black, xvii, 135, 195
  Tuscan Black, Soup, 210
Caglione, Gaetana, 17–20, *18*, 22, 24–25
Cake
  Apple, 126–27
  Fruitcake (*Panforte*), 170–71
  Pastry Cream and Fruit–Filled Sponge,
    190–91
  Rice, 128–29
Capanni, Graziella, 17–20, *18*, 22, 24–25
Caper(s), 135–36
  Tuna, Potato, and, Salad, 111
Castello Banfi, *xvii*, 117, 124
Catamario, Adalgisa and Eduardo,
    37–39, *38*
Certaldo, Paolo, 86
Cheese
  Buccellato with Strawberries and
    Mascarpone, 68
  buffalo mozzarella, 134
  Crustless Green Vegetable Pie, 209
  Iris's Tuscan Meatballs, 77–78
  Lulu San Angelo's Ricotta, Meatballs,
    79
  marzolino, 146
  on menu, as separate course, 61
  Olive Pizza, 31
  Onion Soup, 206
  Parmigiano-Reggiano, 11, 206
  Pecorino with Black Peppercorns in
    Olive Oil, 152
  Pecorino, and Fava Beans, 154
  Pecorino, for Pesto, 41
  Penne with Butter and Truffle Paste,
    189
  Penne with Ricotta, Sauce, 161
  Potato Gnocchi with Pecorino Cream
    Sauce, 148–49
  Salad with Four, 76
  Spinach and Ricotta, Gnocchi, 150–51
  substitutes for Italian, 76
  taleggio, 76, 134
  Tuscan pecorino, aged and young, 61,
    76, 134–35, 152
Chef Goes to Tuscany, A, 181–91
  Grilled Eggplant and Green Bean
    Salad, 187
  Grilled Sea Bass, 185–86
  Pastry Cream and Fruit-Filled Sponge
    Cake, 190–91
  Penne with Butter and Truffle Paste,
    189
  Potato and Cherry-Tomato Salad, 188
Chicken
  Breasts in White Wine, 24
  Cooked Under Bricks, 42
  Little Black Toasts with Chicken Liver
    Spread, 99
Chocolate Cookies, 25–26

Cibreo's Yellow Pepper Soup, 205
Classic Fish Stew from Livorno, 110
Conte, Ralph, 183–84, 187–88
Cookies
  Almond, from the Antonio Mattei
    Pastry Shop, 49–50
  biscuit-making in Prato, 48
  Chocolate, 25–26
  Little Horses, 172
  Siena-Style Almond, 178–79
Creamed Leeks, 11
Crustless Green Vegetable Pie, 209

Datini, Francesco di Marco, 47–48
Da Ventura, 53–56, *55*
Desserts
  Apples with Raspberry Sauce,
    140
  Buccellato with Strawberries and
    Mascarpone, 68
  cantucci, xvii, 169
  Fried Apple Rings, 127
  fruit as, in restaurants, 61
  Powdered Sugar Strips, 173–74
  ricciarelli, *169*
  Stuffed Figs Davanzati Style, 87
  sweets of Siena, 168–69
  typical Tuscan, 61
  wine (Vin Santo), 48, 211
  See also Cake; Cookies
Dinner in a Palazzino, 69–81
  Beans Cooked in a Flask, 74
  Iris's Pasta Fantasia with Fresh
    Cannellini Beans and Olive Sauce,
    80
  Iris's Tuscan Meatballs, 77–78
  Lulu San Angelo's Ricotta Cheese
    Meatballs, 79
  pasta with beans, 72, *73*, 80
  Salad with Four Cheeses, 76
  Soup for the Lombards, 81
  Stewed Beans, 75

Eggplant, Grilled, and Green Bean Salad,
    187
Enoteca La Sosta del Rosellino (wine
    bar), 145–47, 153
Escarole and Beans, 207

Falvo, Ettore, 211–12
Farro, 2, 9
Fava beans, 8–9
  Pecorino Cheese and, 154
Fennel
  dried sausage, 61, 134, 211
  flower or pollen, 57
  Mixed Vegetables, 44
  rub for roasted pork, 56–57
Figs, Stuffed, Davanzati Style, 87

Fish
  Classic, Stew from Livorno, 110
  Grilled Sea Bass, 185–86
  Maria Pia and, 107
  Maria Pia's Tuna Paté, 109
  Nancy's Tuna and Olive Spread, 100
  Stewed Red Mullet, 113
Francesca, Piero della, 53
Fredi, Bartolo di, 34
Fremura, Alberto, 54
Fried Apple Rings, 127
Fruit
  Apples with Raspberry Sauce, 140
  Buccellato with Strawberries and
    Mascarpone, 68
  as dessert course, eating, 61
  Fried Apple Rings, 127
  Fruitcake (*Panforte*), 170–71
  Pastry Cream and, –Filled Sponge
    Cake, 190–91
  Stuffed Figs Davanzati Style, 87
Fruitcake (*Panforte*), 170–71
  about, xvii, 168–69

Garlic
  Pesto, 41
  for pork roast, 56
  in rub for grilling, 38
  in Vinegar, 198
Gherardesca, Ricciardetto della, 169
Ginger, Stuffed Zucchini with, 139
Gnocchi
  methods of making, 145–47
  Potato, with Pecorino Cream Sauce,
    148–49
  Spinach and Ricotta Cheese, 150–51
Gorelli, Maria, 117–19, *118*, 126–28
Grape(s), 124
  Harvest Bread, 124–25
  Sweet Pork Sausage with, 59
Grilled Eggplant and Green Bean Salad,
    187
Grilled Sea Bass, 185–86
Grilled T-Bone Steak, *38*, 40

Ham (*proscuitto*)
  Leek Tart, 12–13
  Peas Florence Style, 137
  Penne with Butter and Truffle Paste,
    189
Herbs
  adding during cooking, 159
  basil, keeping green, 41
  Basil and Pine-Nut Sauce, 41
  Beans Cooked in a Flask, 74
  Chicken Breasts in White Wine,
    24
  Grape Harvest Bread, 124–25
  Grilled Sea Bass, 185–86

Little Diced-Tomato-and-Herb Toasts, 98
rosemary, 38–40, 58
sage, popularity of, 9, 197
Salted Pizza Bites, 175
Soup for the Lombards, 81
Spinach and Ricotta Cheese Gnocchi, 150–51
Stewed Beans, 75
tarragon, 197
Tuscan, Rub, 200
used in Tuscany, 9, 197
Wild Boar in Wine, 20–21

In Michelangelo's Neighborhood, 143–54
gnocchi, 145–47
Pecorino with Black Peppercorns in Olive Oil, 152
Pecorino Cheese and Fava Beans, 154
Potato Gnocchi with Pecorino Cream Sauce, 148–49
Ribbon Noodles with Orange and Lemon Zest, 153
Settignano, 145, 147
Spinach and Ricotta Cheese Gnocchi, 150–51
wine sampling, 147
In the Shadow of the Medici, 131–40
Apples with Raspberry Sauce, 140
foods in the Mercato, 134–36
Mercato Centrale, 133–36, *134*
Peas Florence Style, 137
Piazza di San Lorenzo, 133
Practicing *Al Fresco*, 141–42
Spinach with Cream Sauce, 138
Stuffed Zucchini with Ginger, 139
Iris's Pasta Fantasia with Fresh *Cannellini* Beans and Olive Sauce, 80
Iris's Tuscan Meatballs, 77–78

Jenkins, Nancy Harmon, 91–93, 96, 98–100

Kale
Crustless Green Vegetable Pie, 209
Tuscan Black Cabbage Soup, 210

Lago Trasimeno, 101
Lally, Paul, 33
La Selve winery, 211
Leaning Tower of Pisa, 107
Leek(s), 8, 11, 13
Creamed, 11
Tart, 12–13
Tomato Bread Soup, 204
Lemon
Grilled Sea Bass, 185–86

Powdered Sugar Strips, 173–74
Ribbon Noodles with Orange and, Zest, 153
Little Black Toasts with Chicken Liver Spread, 99
Little Cubed Bread Sauce, 121
Little Diced-Tomato-and-Herb Toasts, 98
Little Horses (*Cavallucci*), 172
Lodovici, Iris and Gioni, 71–73, *73*, 79
Lucca's Legacy, 63–68
Buccellato with Strawberries and Mascarpone, 68
Raisin-Anise Bread, 67
ring-shaped sweet bread (*buccellato*), 66–67
Lulu San Angelo's Ricotta Cheese Meatballs, 79

Maria Pia's Pleasing Paté, 105–13
Classic Fish Stew from Livorno, 110
Maria Pia's Tuna Paté, 109
Stewed Red Mullet, 113
Tomatoes Stuffed with Tuna, 112
Tuna, Potato, and Caper Salad, 111
Marinated Green Tomato Salad, 201
Mayonnaise, 109
Meat
beef from *Chianina* cow, 38
grilled, basic Tuscan, xvii
Grilled T-Bone Steak, *38*, 40
Iris's Tuscan Meatballs, 77–78
Lulu San Angelo's Ricotta Cheese Meatballs, 79
preparation tips, 24
raw-cured wild boar, 211
Roasted Pork Da Ventura Style, 56–57
as second course, 61, 77
Stuffed Zucchini with Ginger, 139
Sweet Pork Sausage with Grapes, 59
Tuscan dried sausage, 61, 134, 211
Venison Stew Cooked in Red Wine, 122–23
Wild Boar in Wine, 20–21
Meatballs, 79
Iris's Tuscan, 77–78
Lulu San Angelo's Ricotta Cheese, 79
Medici family, 133
Merchant of Prato, The (Origo), 47
Merchant of Prato's Biscuits, The, 45–50
Almond Cookies from the Antonio Mattei Pastry Shop, 49–50
biscuit making, 48, 49
Michelangelo, 145, 147
Minding My Garden, 193–212
author's garden, 195–97, *196*
cherry tomatoes, drying, 196

Cibreo's Yellow Pepper Soup, 205
Crustless Green Vegetable Pie, 209
dressing for Italian salads, 196
Escarole and Beans, 207
Garlic in Vinegar, 198
herbs, used in Tuscany, 197
Marinated Green Tomato Salad, 201
Mixed Greens Salad, 202
Onion Soup, 206
salad, as course in Italy, 195
Small Onions in Vinegar, 199
Summer Bread Salad, 203
Tomato Bread Soup, 204
Tuscan Black Cabbage Soup, 210
Tuscan Herb Rub, 200
Zucchini Tart Viareggio Style, 208
Miniera, Damiano and Silvia, 145–48, *146*, 152–53
Mint, 8
Spinach and Ricotta Cheese Gnocchi, 150–51
Mindful Gardener, The, 5–13
Braised Artichokes, 10
Creamed Leeks, 11
Leek Tart, 12–13
See also Trapassi, Tergo
Mixed Greens Salad, 202
Monte Maggio, 92
Mushroom(s), 91, *92*, 135
Iris's Tuscan Meatballs, 77–78
Wide Noodles with Mixed, Sauce, 159
My Big, Fat Tuscan Pizza(s), 27–32, *30*
Basic Pizza Dough, 32
Olive Pizza, 31

Nancy's Tuna and Olive Spread, 100
Nancy's Tuscan Bread, 96–97
Nannini (pastry shop), 167–69, *168*
Nuts
Fruitcake (*Panforte*), 170–71
Little Horses (*Cavallucci*), 172
Pesto, 41
Pine Nut Sauce, 164
Siena-Style Almond Cookies, 178–79
Stuffed Figs Davanzati Style, 87
Walnut Sauce, 162

Olive(s)
Iris's Pasta Fantasia with Fresh *Cannellini* Beans and, Sauce, 80
Nancy's Tuna and, Spread, 100
Penne with Uncooked Tomato-, Sauce, 160
Pizza, 31
Olive Oil
Little Cubed Bread Sauce, 121
Pecorino with Black Peppercorns in, 152
Tuscan, 135

Onion(s)
  Mixed Vegetables, 44
  Small, in Vinegar, 199
  Soup, 206
Orange
  Little Horses, 172
  Powdered Sugar Strips, 173–74
  Ribbon Noodles with, and Lemon
    Zest, 153
  Siena-Style Almond Cookies, 178–79
Origo, Iris, 47

Palazzo Datini, Prato, 47
Palazzo Davanzati, Florence, 83–87
Palazzo Vecchio, 141
Pasta, 77
  Basil and Pine-Nut Sauce, 41
  Cherry Tomato–Pesto Sauce, 43
  cooking instructions, 23
  as first course, 61
  Iris's, Fantasia with Fresh *Cannellini*
    Beans and Olive Sauce, 80
  makers of (*sfoglina*), 54
  Penne with Butter and Truffle Paste,
    189
  Penne with Ricotta Cheese Sauce,
    161
  Penne with Uncooked Tomato-Olive
    Sauce, 160
  pinci, 117–19, *118*, 135
  Ribbon Noodles with Orange and
    Lemon Zest, 153
  tagliatelle, 135, 153
  Thick Noodles (*Pinci*), 119–20
  tradition of making at home, 54
  Tuscan preference, penne, 189
  type used with beans, 72, *73*, 80
  Walnut Sauce, 162
  Wide Homemade Noodles, 22–23,
    135
  Wide Noodles with Mixed Mushroom
    Sauce, 159
Pastry Cream and Fruit–Filled Sponge
    Cake, 190–91
Pea(s)
  Florence Style, 137
  Tuscan Beef Stew, 123
Peach(es), white, 135
Pecorino, 9, 61, 76, 134–35, 152
  with Black Peppercorns in Olive Oil,
    152
  caciotta, 61
  Cheese and Fava Beans, 154
  marzolino, 61, 146
  Olive Pizza,
Penzey's catalog, 57
Pepper, Cibreo's Yellow, Soup, 205
Peppercorns, Pecorino with Black, in
    Olive Oil, 152

Pesto, 41
  Cherry Tomato–, Sauce, 43
Pia, Maria, 107–9, *108*, 112–13
Piazza Signoria, Florence, 141–42
Pie, Crustless Green Vegetable, 209
Pine Nuts
  Cherry Tomato–Pesto Sauce, 43
  Pesto, 41
  Sauce, 164
Pizza
  Basic, Dough, 32
  Olive, 31
  Salted, Bites, 175
Pork, 38, 54–55, *55*
  dried sausage, 61, 134, 211
  Italian, 56
  marinating belly cut, 56
  Roasted, Da Ventura Style, 56–57
  rub of fennel flower, 55
  Sweet, Sausage with Grapes, 59
  thinly sliced, cured, 147
Potato(es)
  and Cherry-Tomato Salad, 188
  Cibreo's Yellow Pepper Soup, 205
  gnocchi, 145–47
  Gnocchi with Pecorino Cream Sauce,
    148–49
  Maria Pia's Tuna Paté, 109
  Mixed Vegetables, 44
  with Olive Oil and Rosemary, 58
  Tuna, and Caper Salad, 111
Poultry. *See* Chicken
Puccini, Giacomo, 65–66

Raisin
  -Anise Bread, 67
  Rosemary and, Rolls, 176–77
Raphael Bar Bistro, 193
Raspberry(ies)
  Apples with, Sauce, 140
  tip for storing, 140
Red Mullet, 108
  Stewed, 113
Restaurants
  bill, 61–62
  bread and cover charges, 60–61
  Cibreo, 205
  courses served in, 61
  Da Ventura, 53–56, *55*
  Enoteca La Sosta del Rosellino (wine
    bar), 145–47, 153
  menu items, common, 60–62
  menus posted, 60
  open air, 141–42
  Raphael Bar Bistro, 193
  ratings, 53
  tipping, 62
Ribbon Noodles with Orange and
    Lemon Zest, 153

Rice
  arborio, 128, 136
  Cake, 128–29
  expert, Edgardo Sandoli, 128
Roasted Pork Da Ventura Style, 56–57
Rosemary, 38–39
  Grape Harvest Bread, 124–25
  Grilled Sea Bass, 185–86
  Potatoes with Olive Oil and, 58
  and Raisin Rolls, 176–77
  Salted Pizza Bites, 175
  Tuscan Herb Rub, 200
Rossellino, Antonio Gamberelli del, 145
Rossellino, Bernardo, 152

Sage, 9, 197
  Beans Cooked in a Flask, 74
  Chicken Breasts in White Wine, 24
  Soup for the Lombards, 81
  Spinach and Ricotta Cheese Gnocchi,
    150–51
  Stewed Beans, 75
  Wild Boar in Wine, 20–21
Salad
  with Four Cheeses, 76
  greens with beefsteak, *38*, 40
  Grilled Eggplant and Green Bean, 187
  lettuces, 203
  Marinated Green Tomato, 201
  on menu, as course, 61
  Mixed Greens, 202
  Potato and Cherry-Tomato, 188
  Summer Bread, 203
  Tuna, Potato, and Caper, 111
San Angelo, Lulu, 79
Sandoli, Edgardo, 128
San Sepolcro's Secrets, 51–59, *55*
  Potatoes with Olive Oil and
    Rosemary, 58
  Roasted Pork Da Ventura Style, 56–57
  Sweet Pork Sausage with Grapes, 59
Sauce
  Basil and Pine Nut, 41
  bread in, 92, 118
  Cherry Tomato–Pesto, 43
  Fresh Tomato, 163
  Little Cubed Bread Sauce, 121
  Mixed Mushroom, 159
  Olive, 80
  Pecorino Cream, 148–49
  Pine-Nut, 164
  Raspberry, 140
  Ricotta Cheese, 161
  Uncooked Tomato-Olive, 160
  Walnut, 162
  white cream, 138
Sauce Sense, 155–64
  fish, 157
  Fresh Tomato Sauce, 163

Penne with Ricotta Cheese Sauce, 161
Penne with Uncooked Tomato-Olive
  Sauce, 160
Pine Nut Sauce, 164
thick or thin, rule of thumb, 158
Walnut Sauce, 162
white cream, 157
Wide Noodles with Mixed Mushroom
  Sauce, 159
Sea Bass, Grilled, 185–86
Siena-Style Almond Cookies, 178–79
Signature Sweets of Siena, 165–79
  Almond Cookies, 178–79
  Fruitcake, 168–69, 170
  Little Horses (*Cavallucci*), 172
  Powdered Sugar Strips, 173–74
  Rosemary and Raisin Rolls, 176–77
  Salted Pizza Bites, 175
Small Onions in Vinegar, 199
Snacks, 136
  Rosemary and Raisin Rolls, 176–77
  Salted Pizza Bites, 175
  Zucchini Tart Viareggio Style, 208
Soares, Donna Petti-, 33
Soup
  Cibreo's Yellow Pepper, 205
  for the Lombards, 81
  Tomato Bread, 204
  Tuscan Black Cabbage, 210
Spannocchia farm, xvii, 1–4, *3*, 7–9, *8*,
  17–19, *18*, 29–30, *30*, 195, 197
Spinach
  Cibreo's Yellow Pepper Soup, 205
  Crustless Green Vegetable Pie, 209
  Florence-Style, in Cream Sauce, 138
  Florentine style and, 138
  and Ricotta Cheese Gnocchi, 150–51
Stew
  Classic Fish, from Livorno, 110
  Tuscan Beef, 123
  Venison, Cooked in Red Wine,
    122–23
  Wild Boar in Wine, 20–21
Stewed Beans, 75
Stewed Red Mullet, 113
Stratton, Francesca Cinelli and Randall,
  1–4, *3*, 17
Strawberries, Buccellato with, and
  Mascarpone, 68
Stuffed Figs Davanzati Style, 87
Stuffed Zucchini with Ginger, 139
Summer Bread Salad, 203
Swiss Chard
  Crustless Green Vegetable Pie, 209

Tart
  dough, 12
  Leek, 12–13
  Zucchini, Viareggio Style, 208

Taste for Saltless Bread, A, 89–100
  bread-making, 92–93
  Little Black Toasts with Chicken Liver
    Spread, 99
  Little Diced Tomato and Herb Toasts,
    98
  Nancy's Tuna and Olive Spread, 100
  Nancy's Tuscan Bread, 96–97
  Teverina, 91–93, *92*
  Tuscan Bread, 94–95
Thick Noodles (*Pinci*), 119–20
To Eat Like a Florentine, 35–44
  Basil and Pine-Nut Sauce, 41
  Cherry Tomato–Pesto Sauce, 43
  Chicken Cooked Under Bricks, 42
  Grilled T-Bone Steak, 40
  Mixed Vegetables, 44
Tofanelli, Giuliano, 53
Tofanelli, Marco, 53–57, *55*
Tomato(es)
  Bread Soup, 204
  Cherry,–Pesto Sauce, 43
  Fresh, Sauce, 163
  Little Cubed Bread Sauce, 121
  Little Diced, -and-Herb Toasts, 98
  Marinated Green, Salad, 201
  Olive Pizza, 31
  Penne with Uncooked, -Olive Sauce,
    160
  Potato and Cherry-, Salad, 188
  salad, choice for, 7
  Soup for the Lombards, 81
  Stewed Beans, 75
  Stewed Red Mullet, 113
  Stuffed with Tuna, 112
  Summer Bread Salad, 203
  Tuscan Beef Stew, 123
  Tuscan Black Cabbage Soup, 210
  Tuscan varieties, 7, 135
  Venison Stew Cooked in Red Wine,
    122–23
Trapassi, Tergo, 2–3, 7–9, *8*, 195, 196
Truffle Paste, Penne with Butter and,
  189
Truslow, Bill, 33
Tuna
  canned, using, 107, 111
  Maria Pia's Tuna Paté, 109
  Nancy's, and Olive Spread, 100
  Potato, and Caper Salad, 111
  Tomatoes Stuffed with, 112
Tuscan Beef Stew, 123
Tuscan Black Cabbage Soup, 210
Tuscan Bread, 94–95
Tuscan cuisine
  basic food products, xvi, xvii
  beefsteak, 38, 40, 60, 134
  beans as staple of, 72
  black cabbage, xvii, 135, 195

bread, flat, 31, 92
bread, grilled, xvii, 61
bread of Lucca, 66–67
bread, saltless, as traditional, 92
cheese, 9, 61
courses, 61
cow breed (*Chianina*), 38, 40
crostini, 99
as *cucina povera*, xvi–xviii, 19, 121,
  212
dessert, fruit as, 61
dried sausage, local, 61, 134, 211
effect of mad cow epidemic, 38
Florentine style, 138
foods in the Mercato Centrale,
  Florence, 134–36
fried apple rings at Carnivale, 127
herbs used in, 9, 197
grilled chicken in, 42
home cooking, 54, 77, 93
knife (*mezzaluna*), 38, 40
menu items, common, 60–62
mushroom-hunting, 91, *92*
olive oil, 135
pasta-makers (*sfoglina*), 54
pastry shops, 31
pecorino, 61, 76, 134–35, 152
penne, preference for, 189
pinci or *pici*, 119
sage, popularity of, 9
soups in, 206
sweets in, xvii, 48, 61
vegetable gardens, xvii
tripe, 134
wild boar, 20, 134
Tuscan festivals
  Carnivale, 127, 173, 208
  San Lorenzo, 12
  San Luca, 42
Tuscan Herb Rub, 200
Tuscan towns and cities
  Arezzo, 183
  Campo, 107
  Cortona, 101–2
  Florence, xvii, 38, 71, 73, 85–86,
    133–36, *134*, 141–42, 205
  Impruneta, 42
  Livorno, 108, 110
  Lucca, 65–66, 67
  Lucignano, 33–34
  Montalcino, *xvii*, 117
  Pienza, 135, 152
  Pisa, xvii, 2, 107
  Prato, 47–48
  San Sepolcro, 53–55
  Settignano, 145, 147
  Siena, xvii, 1, 167–69, 197
  Teverina, 91–93, *92*
  Viareggio, 208

Tuscan wines
  cabernet, 73
  Chianti, xvi, 20
  Gioni Lodovici and, 71–73
  Montalcino region, *xvii*, 117, 152
  sampling, 147
  Sangiovese, 73
  Supertuscans, 147
  Vin Santo, 73, 169, 211

Vegetable(s)
  aromatic, 17, 18, 20
  Braised Artichokes, 10
  Creamed Leeks, 11
  Crustless Green, Pie, 209
  Florence-Style Spinach in Cream
    Sauce, 138
  Grilled Eggplant and Green Bean
    Salad, 187
  Leek Tart, 12–13
  on menu (*contorni*), 61
  Mixed, 44
  Peas Florence Style, 137
  Potatoes with Olive Oil and
    Rosemary, 58
  Small Onions in Vinegar, 199

Stuffed Zucchini with Ginger, 139
Zucchini Tart Viareggio Style, 208
See also Salad; Soup; *specific vegetables*
Venison Stew Cooked in Red Wine,
  122–23
Vinegar
  Garlic in, 198
  Small Onions in, 199
  symbolic meaning to Italians, 198
Vineyard Kitchen, 115–29
  Apple Cake, 126–27
  Fried Apple Rings, 127
  Grape Harvest Bread, 124–25
  Little Cubed Bread Sauce, 121
  making *pinci*, 117–18, *118*
  meal at, 118
  Maria Gorelli, 117–19, *118*, 126–28
  Rice Cake, 128–29
  Thick Noodles (*Pinci*), 119–20
  Tuscan Beef Stew, 123
  Venison Stew Cooked in Red Wine,
    122–23
  Villa Banfi Vineyards, 117, 124

Walnut Sauce, 162
When Tuscan Women Cook, 15–26, *16*

Chicken Breasts with White Wine,
  24
Chocolate Cookies, 25–26
pasta-making, 17–18
wild boar preparation, 17–18
Wide Homemade Noodles, 22–23
Wild Boar in Wine, 20–21
White Sauce, 138
  Crustless Green Vegetable Pie, 209
Wide Homemade Noodles, 22–23
Wide Noodles with Mixed Mushroom
  Sauce, 159
Wild Boar, 17–18, 211
  in Wine, 20–21
Wine
  Centine, 118
  Chicken Breasts with White, 24
  Tuscan Beef Stew, 123
  Venison Stew Cooked in Red,
    122–23
  Wild Boar in, 20–21

Zucchini
  Mixed Vegetables, 44
  Stuffed, with Ginger, 139
  Tart Viareggio Style, 208

Italian Index

Aceto
    Aglio sott', 198
    Cipolline sott', 199
    un segreto dell'aceto, 198
Aglio sott'Aceto, 198
Anelli di Mele, 127
Antipasti
    Cresentine Salate, 175
    crostini, 94
    Crostini Neri, 99
    Crostini Rossi, 98
    Fantasia di Tonno all'Annunziata, 100
    Paté di Tonno alla Maria Pia,
       109
    Pecorino e Fave, 154
    Pecorino con Pepe Nero sott'Olio, 152
    Polpettine alla Iris, 77
    Porrata, 12–13
    Schiacciata alle Olive, 31
Arancia
    Cavalluci, 172
    Cenci, 173–74
    Tagliatelle alle Scorzette di, e Limone, 153
Arugula, 40

Bagnomaria, 128
Basilico
    Pappa al Pomodoro, 204
    Pesto, 41
    Salsa Fresca di Pomodoro, 163

Battuto, 17–18, 20, 38
Besciamella, 72, 138, 157, 209
Biscotti
    brutti ma buoni, 48
    Cavalluci, 172
    di Prato Antonio Mattei, 49–50
    Ricciarelli di Siena, 167, 168, 169, 178
    Salame Dolce, 18, 25–26
Bistecca, 38, 38, 40
    alla Fiorentina, 40
    al sangue, 38, 40, 60, 134
    tagliata, 40
Branzino alla Griglia, 185–86
Bruschetta, 41
Buccellato, 67
    alle Fragole e Mascarpone, 68
    di Lucca, 66–67

Capperi, 135–36
    Fantasia di Tonno all'Annunziata, 100
    Insalata di Tonno, Patate, ei, 111
Capriolo Scottiglia, 122
Carciofi, 8
    morello, 8
    in Umido, 10
Cardi, 7–8
Carne
    Bistecca alla Fiorentina, 38, 38
    Capriolo Scottiglia, 122
    di cavallo, 134

Chianina (vacca), 38, 40
cinghiale, 17, 134, 211
Cinghiale al Vino, 20–21
Cintasenese (porco), 2
Colvana (vacca), 2
Erbe Toscane, 200
finocchiona, 61, 134, 211
Pancetta di Maiale in Porchetta,
    54–57
Polpette di Ricotta alla Lulu San Angelo,
    79
Polpettine alla Iris, 77–78
Pomarancina (pecora), 2
Spezzatino Toscano, 123
stinco di vitello, 55
tagliata, 40
trippa, 134, 212
Casalinga, 54, 77, 93
Cacciucco alla Livornese, 110
Cavalluci, 172
Cavolo Nero, xvii, 135, 195
    Ribollita, 195, 210
Cenci, 167, 168, 169, 173–74
Chef Goes to Tuscany, A, 181–91
    Branzino alla Griglia, 185–86
    Insalata di Melanzane e Fagiolini, 187
    Insalata di Patate e Pomodorini, 188
    Penne al Coccio, 189
    Zuccotto, 190–91
Cinghiale, 17–18, 134

Cinghiale (cont'd)
  prosciutto di, 211
  al Vino, 20–21
Cioccolato
  Salame Dolce, 18, 25–26
  Zuccotto, 190–91
Cipolle (Cipollini), 108, 199
  sott' Aceto, 199
  Zuppa di, 206
Coccio, Penne al, 189
Coltello, mezzaluna, 38, 40
Contorni
  battuto, 20
  Carciofi in Umido, 10
  Cippoline, 108
  Piselli alla Fiorentina, 137
  Scarola e Fagioli, 207
  Scarpaccia Viareggina, 208
  Spinaci alla Fiorentina, 138
  Tuttoinsieme, 44
  Zucchine Ripiene allo Zenzero, 139
Crema di Porri, 11
Cresentine Salate, 175
Crostata
  pasta, 13
  Porrata, 12–13
  Scarpaccia Viareggina, 208
Crostini Rossi, 98
Cucina povera, xvi–xviii, 19, 121, 212

Dinner in a Palazzino, 69–81
  Fagioli al Fiasco, 74
  Fagioli all'Uccelletto, 75
  Insalata con Quattro Formaggi, 76
  Polpette di Ricotta alla Lulu San Angelo, 79
  Polpettine alla Iris, 77–78
  Straccetti, 72, 73, 80
  Zuppa Lombarda, 81
Dolci
  Anelli di Mele, 127
  baba au rhum, 73
  Biscotti di Prato Antonio Mattei, 49–50
  brutti ma buoni, 48
  Buccellato alle Fragole e Mascarpone, 68
  Buccellato di Lucca, 66, 67
  Cavalluci, 172
  cantucci (morselletti), xvii, 167, 168, 169
  Cenci, 167, 168, 169, 173–74
  Mele con la Salsa di Lampone, 140
  Panforte, xvii, 167–71
  Ricciarelli di Siena, 167, 168, 169, 178
  Salame Dolce, 18, 25–26
  la torta mantovana, 48
  Torta di Mele, 126
  Torta di Riso, 128–29
  Tuscan classico, 48, 61

Vin Santo con biscotti, 48
Zuccotto, 190–91

Erbe, 9
  Cinghiale al Vino, 20–21
  Crostini Rossi, 98
  dragoncello, 197
  Fagioli al Fiasco, 74
  Fagioli all'Uccelletto, 75
  mentrasta, 8
  Pan di Ramerino, 176–77
  Patate con Olio e Ramerino, 58
  Pesto, 41
  Petti di Pollo al Vino Bianco, 24
  prezzemolo, 9
  ramerino, 58
  salvia, 9
  Toscane, 200

Fagioli
  cannellini, 72, 74
  fava, 9
  al Fiasco, 72, 74
  Insalata di Melanzane e Fagiolini, 187
  Pecorino e Fave, 154
  Ribollita, 195, 210
  Scarola e, 207
  Straccetti e Cannellini con la Salsa di Olio di Oliva, 80
  toscanelli, 74
  all'Uccelletto, 72, 75
  Zuppa Lombarda, 81
Fantasia di Tonno all'Annunziata, 100
Farro, 2, 9
Fave, Pecorino e, 154
Fettuna, xvii, 61
Fichi Ripieni Davanzati, 87
Finocchio
  fiori di, 55, 57
  Pancetta di Maiale in Porchetta, 54–57
  Tuttoinsieme, 44
Finocchiona, 61, 134, 211
Formaggio
  Buccellato alle Fragole e Mascarpone, 68
  Gnocchi di Patate con Salsa di Pecorino e Panna, 148–49
  Gnocchi di Spinaci e Ricotta, 150–51
  Insalata con Quattro, 76
  mozzarella di bufalo, 134
  Pecorino, 61, 76, 134–35, 152
  Pecorino e Fave, 154
  Pecorino con Pepe Nero sott'Olio, 152
  Penne con la Salsa di Ricotta, 161
  Polpette di Ricotta alla Lulu San Angelo, 79
  taleggio, 134
  Zuppa di Cipolle, 206
Fragole
  Buccellato alle, e Mascarpone, 68

Frutta
  Anelli di Mele, 127
  Buccellato alle Fragole e Mascarpone, 68
  Fichi Ripieni Davanzati, 87
  Mele con la Salsa di Lampone, 140
  Torta di Mele, 126
  Zuccotto, 190–91
Funghi, 91, 92, 135
  brunetta, 91
  ovoli, 91, 135
  Pappardelle con la Salsa di, Misti, 159
  Polpettine alla Iris, 77

Gnocchi, 146–47, 146
  di Patate con Salsa di Pecorino e Panna, 148–49
  di Spinaci e Ricotta, 150–51
  senza farina, 146
Grano, farro, 2, 9

In Michelangelo's Neighborhood, 143–54
  colle armonioso, 145
  enoteca, 145
  gnocchi, 146–47, 146
  Gnocchi di Patate con Salsa di Pecorino e Panna, 148–49
  Gnocchi di Spinaci e Ricotta, 150–51
  Pecorino e Fave, 154
  Pecorino con Pepe Nero sott'Olio, 152
  sosta, 145
  Tagliatelle alle Scorzette di Arancia e Limone, 153
Insalata, 195
  arugula, 40
  di Melanzane e Fagiolini, 187
  Misticanza, 202
  Panzanella, 196, 203
  di Patate e Pomodorini, 188
  pomodori, 7
  di Pomodori Verdi, 196, 201
  con Quattro Formaggi, 76
  di Tonno, Patate, e Capperi, 111
In the Shadow of the Medici, 131–43
  Mele con la Salsa di Lampone, 140
  Piselli alla Fiorentina, 137
  Spinaci alla Fiorentina, 138
  Zucchine Ripiene allo Zenzero, 139
In Umido, 108
  Capriolo Scottiglia, 122
  Carciofi, 10
  Cacciucco alla Livornese, 110
  Cinghiale al Vino, 20–21
  Spezzatino Toscano, 123
  Triglia, 113

Lampone, Mele con la Salsa di, 140
Limone
  Branzino alla Griglia, 185–86

Cenci, 173–74
  Tagliatelle alle Scorzette di Arancia e, 153
Lord and Lady of Spannochia, The, 1–4
  Cintasenese (porco), 2
  Colvana (vacca), 2
  farro, 2
  mezzadria system, 1
  pannòcchia, 3
  Pomarancina (pecora), 2
  strada bianca, 2
Lucca's Legacy, 63–68
  Buccellato alle Fragole e Mascarpone, 68
  Buccellato di Lucca, 66–67
  torta co'becchi, 66

Maiale
  carpaccio di, 147
  Cintasenese (porco), 2
  pancetta, 56
  Pancetta di, in Porchetta, 54–57
  rosticciana, 38–39
  Salsicce con l'Uve, 59
  suino, 38
Maionese, 109
Melanzane
  Insalata di, e Fagiolini, 187
Mandorla, 48
  Biscotti di Prato Antonio Mattei, 49–50
  brutti ma buoni, 48
  la torta mantovana, 48
Maria Pia's Pleasing Paté, 105–13
  Cacciucco alla Livornese, 110
  Insalata di Tonno, Patate, e Capperi, 111
  Paté di Tonno alla Maria Pia, 109
  Pomodori Ripieni con Tonno, 112
  Triglia in Umido, 113
Mele
  Anelli di, *127*
  Fichi Ripieni Davanzati, 87
  con la Salsa di Lampone, 140
  Torta di, 126
Mentrasta, 8
Mercato Centrale, Firenze, 133–35, *134*
Merchant of Prato's Biscuits, The, 45–50
  Biscotti di Prato Antonio Mattei, 49–50
  mandorla, 48
Mezzadria, 1
Mezzaluna, 38, 40, 200
Mindful Gardener, The, 5–13
  campo, 9
  carciofi, 8
  Carciofi in Umido, 10
  cardi, 7–8
  Crema di Porri, 11
  farro, 9
  fava, 9
  pomodori, 7

Porrata, 12–13
  porri, 8
Minding My Garden, 193–212
  Aglio sott'Aceto, 198
  Cipolline sott' Aceto, 199
  Erbe Toscane, 200
  Insalata di Pomodori Verdi, 196, 201
  Misticanza, 202
  Panzanella, 196, 203
  Pappa al Pomodoro, 204
  Passato di Peperoni Gialli, 205
  Ribollita, 195, 210
  Scarola e Fagioli, 207
  Scarpaccia Viareggina, 208
  Torta di Verdure Verdi, 209
  Zuppa di Cipolle, 206
Misticanza, 202
Mortadella
  Polpettine alla Iris, 77
My Big, Fat Tuscan Pizza(s), 27–32
  Margherita Pizza, 30
  Pasta per Pizza, 32
  pizzaiolo, 30
  Schiacciata alle Olive, 31

Noci
  Cavalluci, 172
  Fichi Ripieni Davanzati, 87
  Pesto, 41
  Ricciarelli di Siena, 167, *168*, 169, 178
  Salsa di, 162
  Salsa di Pinoli, 164

Olio d'Oliva
  Patate con, e Ramerino, 58
  Pecorino con Pepe Nero sott', 152
  La Salsa di Briciola, 121
  Straccetti e Cannellini con la Salsa di, 80
  Toscano, 135
Olivo, Schiacciata alle, 31

Palazzo Davanzati, 83–87
  cucina, 85–86
  Fichi Ripieni Davanzati, 87
  loggia, 85
  piano nobile, 85
Pancetta
  di Maiale in Porchetta, 54–57
  Zuppa di Cipolle, 206
Pane, 89–103
  Annunziata, 96–97
  biga, 92
  bruschetta, 41
  casareccio, 93
  Crostini Neri, 99
  Crostini Rossi, 98
  fettuna, xvii, 61, 92
  filone, 93

grano tenero, 92
  La Salsa di Briciola, 121
  Panzanella, 196, 203
  Pappa al Pomodoro, 204
  Schiacciata con l'Uva, 124
  Toscano, 94–95
  Zuppa di Cipolle, 206
  Zuppa Lombarda, 81
Panforte, xvii, 167–71
Pannòcchia, 3
Panzanella, 196, 203
Pappa al Pomodoro, 204
Pappardelle, 22–23
  con la Salsa di Funghi Misti, 159
Passato di Peperoni Gialli, 205
Pasta
  castalingua, 54
  fontana, 22
  Pappardelle, 22–23
  Pappardelle con la Salsa di Funghi Misti, 159
  Penne al Coccio, 189
  Penne ai Pomodori Crudi, 160
  Penne con la Salsa di Ricotta, 161
  Pinci, 117, *118*, 119–20, 135
  Salsa di Pomodori Ciliegini e Pesto, 43
  senza formaggio, 159
  sfoglina, 54
  Straccetti e Cannellini con la Salsa di Olio di Oliva, 80
  tagliatelle, 18, 135, 153
  Tagliatelle alle Scorzette di Arancia e Limone, 153
Pasticerrie, 31
Patate
  Gnocchi di, con Salsa di Pecorino e Panna, 148–49
  con Olio e Ramerino, 58
  Insalata di, e Pomodorini, 188
  Insalata di Tonno, e Capperi, 111
  Ribollita, 195, 210
  Tuttoinsieme, 44
Paté di Tonno alla Maria Pia, 109
Pecorino, 61, 76, 134–35, 152
  caciotta, 61
  e Fave, 154
  Gnocchi di Patate con Salsa di, e Panna, 148–49
  marzolino, 61, 146
  con Pepe Nero sott'Olio, 152
  Schiacciata alle Olive, 31
  taleggio, 76
  Toscano, 152
Penne
  al Coccio, 189
  ai Pomodori Crudi, 160
  con la Salsa di Ricotta, 161
Pepe Nero sott'Olio, Pecorino con, 152
Peperoncini, 135

Peperoni Gialli, Passato di, 205
Pesca bianca, 135
Pesce
    Branzino alla Griglia, 185–86
    Cacciucco alla Livornese, 110
    Fantasia di Tonno all'Annunziata, 100
    Insalata di Tonno, Patate, e Capperi,
      111
    Paté di Tonno alla Maria Pia,
      109
    Pomodori Ripieni con Tonno, 112
    triglia, 108, *108*
    Triglia in Umido, 113
Pesto, 41
    Salsa di Pomodori Ciliegini e, 43
Petti di Pollo al Vino Bianco, 24
Pinci, 117–20, *118*, 135
Pinoli
    Pesto, 41
    Salsa di, 164
Piselli alla Fiorentina, 137
Pizza
    pasta, 31
    Pasta per, 32
    Schiacciata alle Olive, 31
Pollo
    Crostini Neri, 99
    al Mattone, 42
    Petti di, al Vino Bianco, 24
Polpette di Ricotta alla Lulu San Angelo,
    79
Polpettine alla Iris, 77–78
Pomodori
    bombolini, 7
    Capriolo Scottiglia, 122
    Cacciucco alla Livornese, 110
    ciliegini, 118
    Crostini Rossi, 98
    cuore, 7
    Fagioli all'Uccelletto, 75
    Insalata di Patate e Pomodorini, 188
    Insalata di, Verdi, 196, 201
    mele, 7
    Panzanella, 196, 203
    Pappa al, 204
    Penne ai Pomodori Crudi, 160
    pomodorini, 196
    Ribollita, 195, 210
    Ripieni con Tonno, 112
    La Salsa di Briciola, 121
    Salsa Fresca di, 163
    Salsa di, Ciliegini e Pesto, 43
    San Marzano, 7
    Schiacciata alle Olive, 31
    Spezzatino Toscano, 123
    Triglia in Umido, 113
    Zuppa Lombarda, 81
Porri, 8, 11
    Crema di, 11

Pappa al Pomodoro, 204
    Porrata, 12–13
Prezzemolo, 9
    Cinghiale al Vino, 20–21
Prosciutto
    di cinghiale, 211
    Piselli alla Fiorentina, 137
    Porrata, 12–13

Radicchio di Treviso, 135
Ribollita, 195, 210
Ricciarelli di Siena, 167, *168*, 169, 178
Riso
    arborio, 128, 136
    Torta di, 128–29
Ristorante
    al fresca, 141–42
    antipasto 61
    Cibreo, 205
    conto, 61–62
    Da Ventura, 53–56, *55*
    Enoteca La Sosta del Rosellino, 145–47,
      153
    menu, 60–62
    pane e coperto, 60–61
    primo piatto, 61
    secondo piatto, 61
    servizio, 61
Rosmarino [Ramerino]
    Branzino alla Griglia, 185–86
    Cinghiale al Vino, 20–21
    Pan di Ramerino, 176–77
    Patate con Olio e, 58
    spazzola, 39, 40, 58

Salame Dolce, 18, 25–26
Salsa
    Besciamella, 72, 138, 209
    di Briciola, 121
    Fresca di Pomodoro, 163
    Funghi Misti, 159
    di Noci, 162
    Olio di Oliva, 80
    di Pecorino e Panna, 148–49
    Pesto, 41
    di Pinoli, 164
    Pomodori Ciliegini e Pesto, 43
    Pomodori Crudi, 160
    ragu, San Marzano pomodori, 7
    Ricotta, 161
Salsicce
    Finocchiona, 61, 134, 211
    con l'Uve, 59
Salvia, 9
    Capriolo Scottiglia, 122
    Cinghiale al Vino, 20–21
    Fagioli al Fiasco, 74
    Fagioli all'Uccelletto, 75
    Gnocchi di Spinaci e Ricotta, 150–51

Petti di Pollo al Vino Bianco, 24
    Salsa di Noci, 162
    Zuppa Lombarda, 81
San Francesco, Lucignano, 33–34
San Sepolcro's Secrets, 51–59
    Museo Civico, 53
    Pancetta di Maiale in Porchetta, 54
    Patate con Olio e Ramerino, 58
    Salsicce con l'Uve, 59
    sfoglina, 54
Sauce Sense, 155–64
    besciamella, 157
    garum, 157
    Pappardelle con la Salsa di Funghi Misti,
      159
    Penne ai Pomodori Crudi, 160
    Penne con la Salsa di Ricotta, 161
    pesto, 157
    Salsa Fresca di Pomodoro, 163
    Salsa di Noci, 162
    Salsa di Pinoli, 164
Scarola e Fagioli, 207
Scarpaccia Viareggina, 208
Schiacciata con l'Uva, 124
Schiacciata alle Olive, 31
Sfoglina, 54
Signature Sweets of Siena, 165–79
    Cavalluci, 172
    cantucci (morselletti), 167, *168*, 169
    Cenci, 167, *168*, 169, 173–74
    Cresentine Salate, 175
    Pan di Ramerino, 176–77
    panforte, 167–71
    panini, 168
    Ricciarelli di Siena, 167, *168*, 169,
      178
    savoiardi, 168
Spezzatino Toscano, 123
Spinaci
    alla Fiorentina, 138
    Gnocchi di, e Ricotta, 150–51
    Torta di Verdure Verdi, 209
Spuntino, 136
    Cresentine Salate, 175
    Pan di Ramerino, 176–77
Straccetti, 72, *73*
    e Cannellini con la Salsa di Olio di
      Oliva, 80

Tagliata, 40
Tagliatelle, 18, 153
    alle Scorzette di Arancia e Limone, 153
Taste for Saltless Bread, A, 89–103
    Crostini Neri, 99
    Crostini Rossi, 98
    Fantasia di Tonno all'Annunziata,
      100
    Pane Annunziata, 96–97
    Pane Toscano, 94–95

To Eat Like a Florentine, 35–45
  Bistecca alla Fiorentina, 40
  Pesto, 41
  Pollo al Mattone, 42
  Salsa di Pomodori Ciliegini e Pesto, 43
  Tuttoinsieme, 44
Tonno
  Fantasia di, all'Annunziata, 100
  Insalata di, Patate, e Capperi, 111
  Paté di Tonno alla Maria Pia, 109
  Pomodori Ripieni con Tonno, 112
Torta
  di Mele, 126
  di Riso, 128–29
  di Verdure Verdi, 209
  Zuccotto, 190–91
Triglia, 108, *108*
  in Umido, 113
Tuttoinsieme, 44

Un'orto, xvii
Uve
  Salsicce con l', 59
  Schiacciata con, 124

Vineyard Kitchen, 115–29
  Anelli di Mele, *127*
  bagnomaria, 128–29
  Capriolo Scottiglia, 122
  Pinci, 117, *118*, 119–20
  La Salsa di Briciola, 121
  Schiacciata con l'Uva, 124
  Spezzatino Toscano, 123
  Torta di Mele, 126
  Torta di Riso, 128–29
  vendemmia, 124
Vino
  Capriolo Scottiglia, 122
  Chianti, 20, 37
  "Cin cin!," 118
  Cinghiale al, *20–21*
  DOGCO, 37
  Montalcino, xvii
  Petti di Pollo al Vino Bianco, 24
  Spezzatino Toscano, 123
  Vin Santo, 48, 211–12

When Tuscan Women Cook, 15–26
  battuto, 17–18, 20

cinghiale, 17–18
Cinghiale al Vino, 20–21
Pappardelle, 22–23
Petti di Pollo al Vino Blanco, 24
Salame Dolce, 18, 25–26
tagliatelle, 18

Zenzero, Zucchine Ripiene allo, 139
Zucca Fiorentina, 135
Zucchine
  Ribollita, 195, 210
  Ripiene allo Zenzero, 139
  Scarpaccia Viareggina, 208
  Tuttoinsieme, 44
Zuccotto, 190–91
Zuppa
  di Cipolle, 206
  Lombarda, 81
  con pane, 92
  Pappa al Pomodoro, 204
  Passato di Peperoni Gialli, 205
  Ribollita, 195, 210